HEDGE PUBLISHERS

**To order
The Profit-Taker Breakthrough call:
1-800-69-HEDGE**

**For more information about
The Profit Taker Seminar Call:
1-800-342-2936**

THE PROFIT-TAKER
BREAKTHROUGH

THE PROFIT-TAKER
BREAKTHROUGH

THE PROVEN
RAPID MONEY-MAKER
IN GOOD AND BAD MARKETS

DON ABRAMS

HEDGE PUBLISHERS

Published by

Hedge Publishers

U.S.
420 Ford St., Box 967
Ogdensburg, New York
13669

CANADA
1974 Baseline, Box 33025
Ottawa, Ontario
K2C 3Y9

The Profit-Taker by Don Abrams copyright © 1978

The Profit-Taker Breakthrough by Don Abrams
copyright © 1995

ISBN 0-9698216-0-3

No part of this book may be reproduced, stored in a retrieval
system or transmitted in any form or by any means, electronic,
mechanical, photocopying, recording or otherwise, except for
purposes of review, without the prior permission of the
publisher.

Readers should use their own judgment and/or consult a
financial expert for specific applications to their individual
situations.

Acknowledgements

I am blessed with a network of great people.

Part of the Cast of Characters:

Companion of my labor of love .... Alie Bolyea
(Certified Obsessive Compulsive -
like me - who has spent count-
less hours on the computer -
editing and researching).

Editor par excellence .... Collett Coverley

Research and inquiry .... Brent Walker

Hedge and investment professionals
(a precious breed!) ....
                              Andrew R. Byneshewsky
                                  Anne-Marie Perron
                                     Yvon Sheridan
                                     David Schultz
                                     David Walter
                                  Vivienne Welchner

Professional proof reader .... Gordon Mallon

Consultants extraordinaire .... Dr. Jim Mullin
                                  Colonel Harold Gold
                                    Wayne Cummings

Computer Consultant....................Derek Levesque

Admonisher .... Gordon Campbell

... God, the source of patience and encouragement, ...

Romans 15:5 (Good News)

CONTENTS

BOOK II

The Profit-Taker Hedge Applied to Other Investments

BOOK III

The Profit-Taker Personal Seminar
or
An In-Depth Example of How the Profit-Taker Hedge is Applied to Stocks and Bonds

BOOK I

HOW THE PROFIT-TAKER HEDGE CREATES RAPID PROFITS IN GOOD AND BAD MARKETS

Chapter 1
The Profit-Taker Model:
The Ultimate Hedge

What makes this book different from the thousands of other "money-making" books?

"How I wish a book such as this had been placed in my hands twenty years ago! What a priceless boon it would have been!" lamented Dale Carnegie about his book How to Win Friends and Influence People - the all time best seller other than the Bible.

Not a modest statement, but it reeks of sincerity. My first reaction to The Profit-Taker Breakthrough might be expected to be the same - for financial reasons. However, if I am to be sincere, I confess I receive enormous pleasure in bringing the good news to the individual investor. For the first time an enlightening model that allows the individual investor to enjoy spectacular profits regardless of whether the trend is up or down is disclosed. Practical and proven strategies that are based on this model will be demonstrated.

The Profit-Taker Breakthrough did not develop like most other books are written. It evolved over almost two decades. It grew as a child grows. The scrutiny and insight of hundreds of investors and seminar participants are reflected in this book. These seminars have been conducted at colleges and universities across Canada and the United States, and even Mainland China.

This book will reveal how large gains in good and bad markets can be made in short periods. This feature is revolutionary. I have found that the people who are most attracted to this strategy are disheartened investors who have been trying to predict which way the market or interest rates are going to go. You will see that no other strategy is as effective as the Profit-Taker regardless of whether the market goes up or goes down.

The degree of risk is ultraconservative. However, the profits are not. Based on the "80"s published recommendations, the results of the Profit-Taker strategies varied from 39 percent to 103 percent, which are exciting considering the fact that the strategies are so conservative. But these results were based on theoretical recommendations, not actual market trades, which is true of most stock market predictions.

Now the substantiating findings are in! Verified trades achieved by eminent and progressive brokers are published in this book for the first time.

There is a myth that if you are satisfied with slightly better than the "bank rate" capital gains, only then can you invest with complete confidence and certainty - that is, you buy "blue-chip", triple A, or government bonds. But never before have markets shown so clearly that even with these conservative investments can you be guaranteed better than "bank rates" gains. Never before has it been shown so clearly that you can lose money slowly over a long period of time. What's so exciting about that?

Conversely, the myth goes that if you pursue the large capital gains, then you take the huge risks. In this book we are going to destroy the myth that "the higher the risk, the higher the potential reward". We'll see how you can make large gains from exciting conservative investments; investments that are more conservative than buying corporate bonds alone.

We'll also discuss how we can "lock-in" profits on relatively short fluctuations, never having that devastating experience of almost reaching your goals and then losing your gain, or even more, because the market changed directions. We are not going to try to take every last dollar out of the market. We'll simply take profits as they occur.

We will see how we can reduce our commissions, in some cases by more than half.

19

I'm not talking about negotiating low commissions with traditional brokers or dealing exclusively with discount brokers. Frankly, this does not always benefit the small investor, as we'll see. But that should not deter anyone from starting with a small amount. Although we are going to be talking about investments such as bonds and real estate, don't think that we are talking about huge amounts of money. Some people have implemented my strategy and done it successfully for under one thousand dollars. We are going to see how we can magnify the amount of money working for you without taking undue risks. And we are not talking simply about borrowing from the bank or your broker.

The Profit-Taker goes far beyond the use of "hedge" techniques. Through a series of short-term and long-term goals, carefully planned in advance, this extraordinary, wonder-working technique can deliver considerable profits through only small fluctuations in the price of common stocks, regardless of whether the fluctuations take place on the downside or the upside.

We're going to see investment situations that do not require any further margin or borrowed money in order to expand the value and reduce the risk. It's worth one hundred times the price of this book! These situations will work very hard for you. Most individual investors are not familiar with the best protective maneuver or investment hedge ideally suited for them. (Often they are influenced by their broker or hairdresser; I don't want to be unfair to brokers, for most are exemplary. We'll talk later about how to tailor the proper one for you. As for the selection of your hairdresser, you're on your own!)

But remember, the people who make the money are those who make their own investment decisions. When you use a strategy based on the the Profit-Taker example and you make money - you know why you did. So you can do it again and again! Should you invest on the basis of a tip and if you are lucky, then you make money - but you know in your heart that it was "the sunny side of the hedge". I have never met a person who can predict which way interest rates or the market will move, and do it consistently. The market is very complex, and is alway constantly reactive to new information: economical, political, environmental, and psychological. If you are working in a vacuum, you may chance upon a good system, but none of us exists that way in the real world. So, why not put yourself in a position to make money on fluctuations regardless of whether the market is up or down. This you will learn here.

What is the profit-taker hedge?

The Profit-Taker Hedge originates from my specific obsession with convertible securities. Convertibles sparked the notion that it was not necessary to take large risks in order to make huge profits. Through research and experience, it became clear to me that since the astute investment houses did not speculate as to which direction the market was to move - let alone a specific stock - I wanted to do the same. As we shall see, the rules are different for the large institutions and the individual investor. Both have advantages! I developed the Profit-Taker Hedge for the individual. The Profit-Taker Hedge is an investment strategy and subsequently a set of rules were extracted, that if substantially followed, will allow the individual investor to profit rapidly in good and bad markets.

As I gained more experience with the Profit-Taker, it became evident that the criteria that made the Profit-Taker Hedge so successful with convertible securities could be creatively applied to almost any endeavour of investing. It is a kind of mind-set. Once you fully appreciate the Profit-Taker concept, you can seize "risk-free" opportunities in other areas such as: coins, salary, bank books, real estate, and so on. In Book II we will discuss more specifically how the Profit-Taker Hedge concept may be used as a touchstone to convert almost any area of investing into one of low risk and high profit potential without guessing in which direction the market will move. The only restriction is what your mind cannot conceive. The Profit-Taker approach to investing is truly revolutionary and I hope it inspires positive dreams and actions in your life as it has in mine.

Could You Suggest How to Get the Most Out of This Book?

1. If you wish to get the most out of this book, there is one inescapable rule. Remember that an approach is being unveiled to small investors that may change their monetary philosophy. Change can be uncomfortable.

When I give seminars on the Profit-Taker Hedge, there exists an ambience of excitement best summed up in one participant's comment: "At last, an intelligent investing philosophy without the usual stress of gambling".

But human nature being what it is, there exists a predictable scepticism. Remember, this is the new wave of intelligent investing. Scepticism and anxieties are welcome! But please keep an open mind. I have seen the principles of the Profit-Taker Hedge literally revolutionize the lives of many of my seminar participants.

To illustrate, I'll relate this story: Two taxidermists had stopped before a window in which an owl was on display. They immediately began to criticize the way it was mounted. Its eyes were not natural; its wings were not in proportion with its head; its feathers were not neatly arranged; and its feet could be improved. When they had finished with their criticism, the owl turned his head and winked at them.

So get to know the Profit-Taker Hedge! Then experience the thrill of knowing that it is real and it works. At last there is a better way than merely predicting the direction to the market, regardless of which area of investment you choose.

2. In this book we will be looking at the most reliable sources available. Very often the difference between just reading a book and investment success is knowing where to find specific material and knowing how to interpret it. The Profit-Taker Breakthrough explains the strategy, and gives you a "hands-on" approach, as well.

This pragmatic approach takes the form of a case study that runs through Book III. The case study starts very basically and progresses rapidly, omitting no steps. It is necessary to use a specific area of investment to demonstrate how successful this Profit-Taker Model of Hedging really is. The specific example used in the case study is the Profit-Taker convertible strategy. The results are demonstrated by actual "broker-executed" examples. The case study is often presented in question and answer format to allow investors with varying degrees of experience to read and learn at different speeds. This permits the reader to be actively involved with the Profit-Taker Hedge rather than simply be uplifted by a new theory. At the end of the case study, the reader will actually be in a position to select the securities that will be the most likely candidates to produce large profits, regardless of whether the market moves up or down.

Furthermore, the investor will now possess the Profit-Taker Hedge technique and be able to apply it to other areas of investment. **This is an action book**. "Ideas", said Arnold Glasgow, "ideas not coupled with actions never become bigger than the brain cells they occupy".

3. **Be creative**. By the time you finish this book, you will be in a position to create new and unique opportunities in your favourite area of investments, using the concept of the Profit-Taker Hedge.

4. As you read this book, underscore those sections you find the most relevant to you. Re-read the parts underlined. This will surely make the book live!

5. Consider investing theoretically in the investment of your choice. You are now in possession of the necessary tools to instruct you to make your own selections. Follow them closely. The skills developed in the application of the Profit-Taker Hedge will give you, no doubt, the assurance that you can indeed invest successfully without having to speculate which direction the market will move.

6. Be persistent. "Persistence", said Napoleon Hill, author of the classic <u>Think and Grow Rich</u>. "Persistence is the direct result of habit ... Fear, the worst of all enemies, can be effectively cured by forced repetitions of acts of courage". So if you encounter any area that is not completely clear, don't quit. **Never quit!** There is simply too much to gain by understanding fear. Fear is a natural instinct when contemplating a new approach to investing. Each time you tackle a new idea it is surely "**an act of courage**". No longer will you fear the anxieties of not knowing the direction of your market.

Chapter 2
Stress-Free Diversification:
The Answer to the Expected
Unexpected

What can we learn from the large institutional hedger or arbitragers?

In October 1938, panic swept the Western world. A "news bulletin" announced that little men called Martians whose eyes were black and gleamed like serpents had landed. "The mouth is kind of V-shaped, with saliva dripping from rimless lips that seem to quiver and pulsate." Some listeners thought the invasion of outer space was real. Apparently no one died, but there were many broken bones and miscarriages reported. The 'culprit' was Orson Wells with his radio adaption of <u>The War of the Worlds</u>, which was broadcast as "news".

In October 1987, almost 50 years later, panic swept Wall Street, which went through the worst ten minutes in its history. The news shocked the world and crowded other stories off the front pages. The Dow Jones plummeted 508 points, or twenty two percent. Well respected stocks dropped forty percent, or more.

Little men called "arbitragers", unofficially nicknamed "arbs", had apparently landed and were identified by some, including the Securities

Exchange Commission, as an important cause of the October crisis. Although most of the panic and the wrath of the investors was vociferous by nature, there was one reported killing. A disbarred Kansas City lawyer, who lost nearly his entire multi-million dollar portfolio, walked into a Merrill Lynch office in Miami with a .357 magnum in his briefcase and killed the branch manager, seriously wounded a broker, and then committed suicide. Fear became rampant. Brokers in one office were reported donning buttons labelled: "I am not the Branch Manager!"

Some analysts argue that arbitrage in the form of program trading did not cause the crash, but merely accelerated its speed once the crash had started.

Basically, the "arbitragers" are professional large institution hedgers. They make large sums of money by applying simple rules of thumb every few minutes of every business day. In classic arbitrage, a security is bought on one stock exchange and simultaneously sold on another. The difference, or spread, as it is called, yields a profit for the arbitragers.

Today, one predominant form of arbitrage is called "program trading" because it is managed by computers. Program trading is a hedge that enables large institutions and big investors to earn profits on the small differences that develop between stock prices and related synergistic instruments such as future indexes. (A future index forecasts what the price of a group of stocks will be on a specific date in the future). This includes arbitrage which is one application of program trading.

The U.S. Securities Exchange Commission also reported that some money managers negotiated with brokers to form a "dynamic hedging" package, and this may have fueled the 190-point plunge in the Dow Jones in October, 1989, as well as the 120-point drop in November, 1991.

Now that we understand the necessary nomenclature, what can we learn from the large hedger known as an "arbitrager"? We can learn that few risks are taken with the more classic arbitrage and this technique is becoming more popular all the time. Often the individual clients are encouraged by investment houses to guess with their hard earned money which direction a stock is going to move. Meanwhile, back at the ranch, rather than investing in its own recommendation, the investment house is 'hedging' for its own account. As Richard Croft, Director of Options Investment Service in Toronto, pointed out so perceptively in the <u>Globe and Mail:</u> "Some analysts think that as much as forty percent of all trading on the New York Stock Exchange is, in fact, arbitrage. What's more, both the number and range of participants continue to grow. Many large brokerage houses have entered the business, trading for their own accounts. And institutional investors are getting involved in increasing numbers".

Forty percent of trading is arbitrage? Absurd? Exaggerated? Inconceivable? Of course, you don't have to believe this phenomenon. I am merely quoting a statement by an eminently authoritative and involved source.

In a detailed and well-researched account of Black Monday in 1987, that is outlined in their book Crash, Aibel and Koff state that "during certain critical periods in October, both index arbitragers and portfolio insurers were selling stocks heavily. They accounted for between thirty percent and sixty-eight percent of the total volume in Standard and Poor's 500 stocks, the cream of the market".

Tim Metz, in his revealing treatise of the October, 1987 crash titled Black Monday, confirms this "program trading (hedging) spread like a brush fire because it offered professional money managers a way to rearrange and mix their stock, bond, and cash holdings instantaneously and at big savings . . . . Since 1984, the big trading firms had been using

30

program trading strategies to produce a rapidly increasing stream of risk-free investment income for themselves." Read that again! Risk-free investment income!

Will the opportunities evaporate as more individuals become aware of the profitability and security of hedging?

Will this bonanza be regulated out of existence? Hardly! For one thing, I believe that the hedge, or arbitrage, is the natural metamorphosis of the speculative nature of the market. As soon as the creative and intelligent mind realizes that forecasting the direction of the market is a waste of time, it will change to 'locking-in' profits through hedging techniques.

As we shall see, opportunities to hedge are always available to the intelligent investor who has developed the mind set spelled out in this book. For example, during the American Civil War, the Secretary of the Treasury had difficulty marketing federal bonds to raise money for the North. As a result, there was a rush to hoard gold. In the latter part of 1861, the war was going badly and there were fears that Britain might support the Confederacy. The rush for gold intensified. The Secretary acknowledged the gold drain and recommended a series of taxes. But before they could take effect, the nation's private banks were forced to suspend payments in gold. Two months later, Congress authorized the issue of new greenbacks. As soon as the new paper money was in use throughout the North, gold and silver went into hiding. Frequently, these precious metals were sent to Canada and sold at a premium. For instance, one type of currency arbitrage was to exchange $100.00 U.S. in silver for $97.00 in gold in Canada, which could then be sold in New York for $120.00 in greenbacks. Similarly, whenever reports of Union losses or defeats reached Wall Street, such hedging practices would increase, causing the price of gold to zoom. Many of the "curbstone" brokers mastered the art of arbitrage and were constantly on the alert for new opportunities.

A few years later, the first cable was successfully laid across the Atlantic, tying Wall Street directly with London and other European financial centers. Soon, investors recognized the opportunity to make a profit on the difference in quotations of the same stock on the New York and European markets by taking advantage of the time differences that existed between them.

Arbitragers found a lucrative environment in which to operate. For instance, at the beginning of this century, a young man in his early twenties, earning $5.00 per week, decided to become an expert in hedging. Many years later, as a capitalist and distinguished advisor to

32

presidents of the United States, Bernard Baruch gave this account in his memoirs, <u>My Own Story</u>: "As an office boy at Kohn's, I had acquired the habit of getting downtown an hour or two before the opening of the Exchange to see whether the London quotations offered opportunities for making an arbitrage profit. On Mondays, in particular, I did that to take advantage of possible developments over the weekend.

On the Monday morning that was the beginning of a puzzling day in Northern Pacific, I was standing at the arbitrage desk where London cables were sent and received. Beside me stood Talbot Taylor, one of the better brokers .... Taylor's brown eyes regarded me intently. His face was expressionless. 'Bernie', he said, tapping his lips with the butt end of his pencil, ' are you doing anything in Northern Pacific?' 'Yes', I replied, 'and I'll tell you how to make some money out of it. Buy in London, sell here, and you take the arbitrage profit."

As you see, the concept is the same today as it was almost ninety years ago! Only the form of the strategies change. As long as you understand the hedging rules and use your creative intelligence, there will be no shortage of hedging opportunities.

One astute broker told me recently that program trading as an arbitrage instrument will never be regulated out of existence because it's "wildly" profitable. How profitable is institutional hedging? Consider this second comment from <u>Black Monday</u>. Tim Metz writes: "Since late 1984, and especially during 1987, program trading has become the hottest trend in the investment world. Program traders use computers to instantaneously and simultaneously buy or sell whole portfolios containing scores of hundreds of blue-chip stocks, with values from tens to hundreds of dollars ...."

In this book, I am committed to translating the obviously lucrative techniques of the big trading firm "arbitrager" or hedger into a model that will be adaptable to the needs of the individual investor. In essence, I will teach you to adopt the successful strategies that the investment houses actually use themselves.

Why is the Profit-Taker hedge a breakthrough?

"Most institutions and large investors hedge as a matter of policy," says a portfolio manager in the professional journal <u>Pension World</u>. That is, the people with money are fully aware of the futility of guessing which way the market will move. So what do they do? They hedge!

How do large hedge traders and arbitragers justify not passing these opportunities on to the individual investor? The large hedgers and arbitragers say they are needed in our capitalistic system. They keep things in balance. That is, they will persistently take a nickel here and a dime there, thereby making an important contribution to the way the market functions. By moving stocks from one market to another, these large hedgers continually balance out stocks and allow the individual investors a more efficient climate in which to play "soothsayer". By doing this, these "nickel and dimer's" have become billion-dollar players. Is it really true that all the individual investor should insist on is "let me play, too?" Read on, and you will find that as an individual investor the principle of these strategies may be adapted so as to give you many of the advantages of the large institutions, with even greater flexibility.

Another reason that arbitragers give to individual investors in order to discourage them from hedging, is that commissions would consume most of the profits at the retail level, whereas the large hedgers pay no commissions (or they would simply pay commissions to themselves). This means that the astute individual investor merely has to find situations that are more to their advantage. Read on!

Most individual investors have very little knowledge about hedging, yet hedge funds are the investment vehicle of choice for many multi-millionaires. Barron's report that such prominent and sophisticated investors as the Rothchild's, the Bass Brothers, Boone Pickens, Alfred Taubman, Laurence Tisch, the Pritzher's, and Carlo De Berneditti favor hedge funds.

A cynical view is that the individual investor is deliberately discouraged from seeking out the hedge opportunities because the large hedging institutions and multi-million dollar investors are not anxious to share the resulting high profits that can be made.

Don't despair! Be persistent! The gold ring here is real and is worth going for. Do not be sold the "cop-out" that all there is left for you is the game of guessing in which direction something will move, or paying someone to guess for you.

Furthermore, the small investor has advantages over the more cumbersome large individual and institutional hedgers. The astute and knowledgeable smaller investor is far more flexible, and can maneuver amongst the more thinly traded securities. For instance, individual hedgers normally would have little trouble trading with shares of a corporation selling at ten dollars and with a volume of five thousand shares per day. Whereas the large hedgers maneuver like a Goodyear Blimp. For example, an exhaustive study at the Wharton School of Finance reported that one hundred and thirty six large funds produced an average return of 10.7 percent annually over an eight year period. During the same period, the average share on the New York Stock Exchange appreciated 12.4 percent annually.

It appears that the inflexibility of large transactions can be counterproductive, even in producing average results. Professional managers of large funds have been mockingly labelled as losers and even compared to blindfolded chimpanzees, heavily fortified with martinis, throwing darts at the stock pages.

The Profit-Taker Hedge allows the individual to benefit from this great advantage of maneuverability in a variety of investments.

What is the very "soul" of hedging?

"Put your investments in several places - many places even - because you never know what kind of bad luck you are going to have in this world". Solid advice from The Wall Street Journal? Or was it Barron's? Maybe Money Magazine? Wrong on all accounts. It was the Bible. (Good News Version, Ecclesiastes, Chapter 11; Verse 2)

Around 450 A.D., the <u>Babylonian Talmud</u> had this to say about diversification: "Let every man divide his money into three parts and invest a third in land, a third in business, and a third let him keep in reserve." Fundamentally still sound financial counsel.

The "soul" of hedging is diversification; the intention being to reduce the risk of the transaction, and the Profit-Taker Hedge has evolved from this solid "silver-of-the-earth" advice. The aim here is to further reduce the risk of the diversification, often profiting from fluctuations, regardless of the direction of the market. Remember what Bernard Baruch, the financial advisor to presidents, replied when asked "what will the market do tomorrow?" He astutely replied, "it will fluctuate". Let us benefit from this knowledge.

As we progress, you will see the diversification of the Profit-Taker Hedge. It will take on different configurations, depending on specific strategies and investments.

Often diversification exists in the form of two distinctly different investment securities that are purchased simultaneously to produce a profit or reduce the risk, regardless of the direction of the market. The Profit-Taker strategy set out later in detail in the Case Study is such a combination; other times, the diversification takes the form of two or more properties that reduce the risk or produce a profit within the same investment vehicle. Such examples of synergistic properties within the same investment will be discussed in Book II. For instance, we will apply the rules of the Profit-Taker Hedge to silver and gold coins.

So if you want to benefit from the practices of the flourishing large institutions or "arbitragers", use the stress-free diversification of hedging.

Chapter 3
The Proven Rapid Money-Maker in Good and Bad Markets

How profitable can hedging really be if it does not depend on whether the market trend is up or down?

Once there was a man named Jones, Alfred Winslow Jones. The only investors who kept up with him were friends who joined him in partnership; subsequently, many of them he made millionaires.

After researching a number of technical stock market strategies, Jones decided that the best approach would be the hedge, so that profits could be made regardless of the direction of the market. So he created his own brand of hedging. Basically, he bought stocks that would advance more than the general market, and sold short stocks that would rise less and preferably fall, thus producing profits on the downside. (How the short sale produces profits on the downside is explained in detail in Book III, Lesson 4).

He formed a 'limited partnership' in 1952 with some friends, and this was probably one of the first hedge funds. How well did he do? Over a period of five fiscal years, ending May 31, 1965,

Jones' fund earned 325 percent. The best performance by any mutual fund for the same period was that of the Fidelity Trust Fund, which showed a 225 percent profit. The Standard and Poor's 500 - the "cream of the crop" - managed an 83 percent profit.

Over a period of ten fiscal years, ending at May 31, 1965, Jones' fund made 670 percent. Compare this result with that achieved by the top mutual fund -- the Dreyfus Fund -- for the same period of time: little more than half the profit (358 percent) was accomplished. The Standard and Poor's 500 moved up 222 percent.

There's more to the story! Jones was not adept at forecasting (be suspicious of anybody who says that they are!). He readily admits to miscalculating the direction of the market. Nevertheless, his ability to apply the principles of "hedging" was brilliant.

That's not all! Even though the profits he earned are incredible compared to the best professionally managed mutual funds, the results are understated. Jones' arrangement was that he would receive 20 percent of the realized profits. Considering the performance of the hedge, is it little wonder that no one complained?

Another hedger has made millions so fast that one might assume he may be held in scorn by the business community. He is not afraid to take on the big boys, and spars with partners such as Marshall Field, Phillips Petroleum, and T.W.A. His name is Carl Icahn.

In a moment of revelation, Icahn disclosed a 1.5 million dollar profit from one gratifying situation with Polaroid that involved a combination of convertible bonds and short sales. He insists it was a no-risk situation. Basically, he used the classic full hedge, much like the strategy explained later in detail, (Book III, Lesson 6). Icahn developed his own brand of hedging formulas that left him protected on the downside with the potential for an enormous gain on the upside.

Similarly, Donald Trump reveals his true philosophy in his autobiography, <u>Trump: The Art of the Deal</u>, when he proclaims: "protect the downside and the upside will take care of itself".

It has been my observation that hedging allows a great deal of creativity that results in great success, and it is from these successes that the rules of the Profit-Taker Hedge evolved.

The following story sounds as if it has been contrived to fit the American dream. A man started out with $2,500 in the 1950's. Over the next thirty years he built America's largest independent oil company, Mesa Petroleum, worth close to three billion dollars. He is also a hedger in commodities such as oil and cattle. What is his philosophy? Boone Pickens opens his heart in his revealing autobiography, <u>Boone</u>. "People sometimes get too serious about business," says Boone. "Business isn't life itself: life is tragic, but business is not. There are no disasters in business that you can't avoid - if you see them coming and make the adjustments. If you understand markets, you can do as well in a down market as you can in an up market. Business, like racquet ball is fun." The fact that you "can do as well in a down market as you can in an up market" is captured in a hedge situation in which Boone Pickens was looking at a seven million dollar profit. The commodity he hedged was cattle. But the only thing you can count on is the unexpected - and it happened. The famous meat boycott triggered by consumer groups in 1973 caused beef prices to collapse. And in Pickens' own words: "Our profit of seven million dollars was, in fact, because of the hedge. Had we not hedged, we would have lost ten million dollars."

The rules of the hedge are the same for the individual as for the multi-millionaire and large investment institutions. The anticipated percentage of profit can even be higher! This will be illustrated by actual hedging trades made by leading brokerage houses published and reproduced in Book I, Chapter 8. and the

Appendices As you'll see, only the strategies - not the rules - have to be adjusted to the type of investment in an appropriate way as you work through the book. You'll see there is no shortage of hedging strategies. So if you want to profit with little or no risk,

Rule 1 is:
Don't waste your time and money trying to predict the direction of the market.

Chapter 4
Disciplined Hedging or "Don't Overstay the Market"

Henry Ford was often asked: "How can I make my life a success?" He would always reply, "if you start something, finish it!"

Ford had worked long but exhilarating hours in a little wood building behind his home. He had a plan to build his home. He had a plan to build his first car. Initially, his enthusiasm kept him within the confines of his original plan, so much so, that he hardly took time to sleep or eat. Then, before he had completed the first Ford automobile, he became acutely aware that he could build a better one. Ford felt certain he could create a second car that would be superior to his first. The thrill and exhilaration of the first planned car diminished.

Why finish one project when you already know you could create a superior one? Ford innately knew the importance of discipline, so he pressed on to complete what he had begun. As a result, he learned more about his second project to construct a car by finishing every detail of his original dream. In addition, he learned a fantastic principle - being sufficiently disciplined to complete what you start opens doors that were previously unknown. Had he succumbed to the allure of constantly modifying his plan, he might never have built a car at all. A similar question is sometimes asked of famous Wall Street author, Martin Zweig: "What traits do investors need to have if they want to succeed in the market?" Zweig answers: "I tell them discipline is the most important - the discipline to follow your method or system and not give in to all the temptations that might weaken your resolve."

Often the typical investor not only fails because of an undisciplined approach to investing; he also fails to see what improvements are necessary in order to create a superior plan.

Hedging is a plan: a plan to reduce the risk or as carried further in the Profit-Taker Hedge - to profit from price fluctuations, regardless of the direction of the market. For instance, the head of Sears Mortgage hedging operations is a disciplined hedger named Sy Naqvi. He is in charge of hedging $5.8 billion in loans originating through Sears Mortgage's vast operations. Naqvi revealed to Mortgage Banking that "we don't try to outguess the market. When you do that you're bound to lose." Further on the publication concluded that "Naqvi worships discipline as the key to successful hedging." Without discipline applied to a sound plan, there can be no consistent prosperity.

Seminar participants often ask me

"doesn't it take a great deal of time to set up a plan to profit regardless of whether the market goes up or down?" Emphatically, "NO"! There is a sense of security in knowing that your decision to buy or sell has been decided in advance, thereby assuring you of a profit on the fluctuations. It is very stressful indeed to lie awake at night pondering what your next investment move is going to be. The wisdom of Ecclesiastes 10:10 (Good News version) rings true: "If your axe is dull and you don't sharpen it, you have to work harder to use it. It is smarter to <u>plan</u> ahead." Define and sharpen each step toward your financial goal. Rules of the Profit-Taker Hedge will raise you above the mass of investors who drift aimlessly.

So to "lock-in" gains and avoid overstaying the market.

<u>Rule 2 is:</u>
Plan to profit from small fluctuations.

Chapter 5
Leverage: Magnify the Money Working For You

What is leverage and how does it apply to hedging?

You probably discovered the power of leverage when you were a youngster. Remember once when playing on a teeter-totter and you learned how to scare bigger kids by poising them in the air, you discovered the advantage of the "longer end" - or leverage.

In investing, the "longer-end" is simply the use of borrowed funds or margin accounts in order to make greater profits. Sometimes, ingenious devices that represent only a small portion of the real value of the underlying security are created, usually for a predetermined time period, such as the case with options. More than seventy percent of these "time conditional" securities are not exercised.

However, leverage when hedging can be "user-friendly". Ordinarily, when an investor is persuaded to guess as to which direction an investment will move, leverage only magnifies the profits and the losses. When you win, you win big. The bank or investment house is not your partner here, they share in neither your

51

profits nor in your losses. So leverage in this situation is neither good nor bad, but simply a tool to amplify the speculation. But with a true hedge situation, risk can be accurately measured at the time the investment is transacted. This risk is often the "spread" or difference between the security which produces the profit if the market moves up, and the security that is defensive (or even produces a profit on the down side). Such Profit-Taker hedges are discussed in detail in Book II and Book III.

Leverage in a hedge situation can even reduce the risk of an investment, as in the case of the convertible security (produces a profit on the upside) and the short sale (produces profit on the down side).

Many investment houses now require only the risk money, or premiums, to be deposited; this premium is the difference between the convertible and the value of the underlying securities the convertible represents. This is a sensible arrangement for the hedge, as any risk can be calculated in advance. Consequently, in such hedge situations, the leverage can magnify the profits, while keeping risk within appropriate limits.

The distinguished Canadian Business and IBC Review revealed that "businessmen who understand the advantages of hedging will bank more and more with bankers who understand hedging. The reason is evident: hedging protects money against price risk; and money that is protected is, increasingly, borrowed money".

The golden rule of leverage is to never borrow more than you need in order to control your investment during the worst scenario. Never, never, never, put yourself in a position where you must dissolve an investment plan that is reacting to the current market situation as expected. The real power of leveraging a true hedge situation is that you can determine the risk of the spread in advance, thereby the borrower should never be in the position known as "overextended". Remember, the more you need money, the harder it is to borrow, and the higher the interest seems to soar. Donald Trump reiterates this principle in his best selling autobiography <u>Trump: The Art of the Deal</u>, when he states: "the best thing you can do is deal from strength, and leverage is the biggest strength you have. Leverage is having something the other guy wants. Or better yet, needs. Or best of all, can't do without.....Leverage: don't make a deal without it."

So if you want to deal from strength:

<u>Rule 3 is:</u>
Use leverage to your advantage.

Chapter 6
Volatility: The Erogenous Zone
of Investing

What is Volatility?

Volatility is like magnifying the amount of your investment without any further cost to you. For our purposes, volatility is simply the price action of the stock or investment over a specific period of time. By converting the volatility of an investment to a percentage we can compare one investment with another.

For instance, when you apply The Profit-Taker Model to a hedge situation, you are not trying to predict the direction of the market. The reason my recommendations and other hedge techniques have such amazing results, in spite of the market being dull or moving sideways is due largely to volatility. Remember, you are not guessing when you apply the Profit-Taker Rule of Volatility. You are not predicting by finding investments that are characteristically active. Like the colour of your eyes, it is the nature of some investments to be far more volatile than others. Certain investments are very conservative in price movement. For instance, Some utility companies are predictably very slow with regard to the movement or volatility of their stock.

Other investments characteristically are very active, and as you will see, you will no longer be afraid of the movement of the stock or investment going in the wrong direction.

Consequently, you want price action, and the more action (or volatility) the greater the profit percentage. Now you welcome action because you are in a very secure strategy because you have applied the Profit-Taker Rules. The thing you don't want is a slow-moving, sluggish investment. By using the Rule of Volatility to the utmost you are condensing "time", allowing your strategy to materialize at full speed. You are no longer afraid of price movement. The greater the action, the more capital gains you'll make. So look deliberately for the most active investment you can find, and then combine this with the other Profit-Taker criteria.

Volatility is much like the momentum that a train gathers up. It doesn't suddenly stop. The momentum carries the train further along. Price action is no different. The mistake made by most investors is trying to predict which direction the stock is going to move.

The manner in which pure price action may be calculated is described in the Profit-Taker case study in Book III, Lesson 8. The volatility of any other investment for the purpose of selecting the most active security, whether it be coins, real estate, or closed-end mutual funds, may be calculated in a similar manner.

Is there a connection between the volatility of an investment and the unpopularity of an investment?

It has been my experience over the years when selecting the most volatile recommendations of the month, that when an investment has a high volatility factor, it is nearly always an unpopular investment and thus is selling at a low point of its trading range. Buying into such an investment against the "herd" is often an act of courage and requires a degree of self-discipline; yet, it has proven to be one of the most fruitful and potentially profitable strategies. The concept of "contrarianism" is as close to buying low and selling high as the investor is going to find and constitutes a true bonus when combining volatility with the 'hedge' techniques described in this book. The most truly volatile situations are often those that are close to their low and are about to turn around.

John Train, in his well-researched book, The Money Masters, (after studying the philosophies and lives of the most successful investors), comes to the conclusion that "since buying what the crowd spurns and selling that which the crowd craves is the essence of the master investor's act, it follows that he must be serenely able to do the opposite of the herd, even though the herd instinct is the strongest human emotion". The Profit-Taker Rule of Volatility shows you how to act against the herd, and do so with confidence.

The celebrated John Templeton, who turned a few thousand dollars into eight mutual funds worth more than $300 million, discovered the value of contrary investing when he was a youngster. He was poor, but bright, and worked his way through college, winning a Rhodes Scholarship to Oxford. John Train uncovered this early story of Templeton, which reveals the essence of his contrary investment philosophy: one day in 1939, just after the war had broken out in Europe, a young man named John Templeton called his broker at Fenner & Beane and gave one of the oddest and most annoying orders a broker could ever hope to receive: "I want you to buy me a hundred dollar's worth of every single stock on both major exchanges that is selling for no more than a dollar a share...".

After a while the broker reported that he had bought Templeton a hundred dollar's worth of every such stock on both exchanges that was not entirely bankrupt. "No, No," said Templeton, "I want them all. Every last one, bankrupt or not." Grudgingly the broker went back to work and finally completed the order. When it was completed, Templeton had a junk pile of 104 stocks in roughly $100 lots, of which 34 were bankrupt. He held on to each stock for the average of four years before selling. The result was no joke at all: he got over $40,000 for the whole potpourri, four times its cost.

After the Second World War, Templeton insisted on buying only those stocks that were out of favour, and then holding them for an average of four years. He purchased an investment firm with eight clients for $5,000. With the impetus of his "contrary" investments success, he rose from obscurity to become a financial legend within his lifetime.

One of the original contrarians was the English economist J. M. Keynes (1883-1946). Mostly as a result of his efforts during the Great Depression, he made about $10 million trading stocks and bonds. His strategy was to select a few unpopular securities that were financially sounder than their market price indicated. Like Templeton, he would hold these stocks in relatively large units for a number of years.

Gerald Loeb summed up the contrary principle superbly as related in Ralph Martin's fascinating book, <u>The Wizard of Wall Street: The Story of Gerald M. Loeb:</u> "The way I look at it, is that one should buy some active well-known stock when people do not want it. Unpopularity, is of course, called for when one is trying to pick

an attractive long-term bargain. Such stocks
that have a broad market are the best candidates
for going up 100%". Loeb stressed that when
defining an ideal investment the business should
be poor. He believed that the best investment
value was available when the worst scenario was
perceived. Fear then prevents the majority of
buyers from taking advantage of low prices.

In order to increase your leverage without
further risk and achieve the best investment
value:

<u>Rule 4 is:</u>
Use volatility (price action) to condense time.

Chapter 7
Commissions: Reduce Commissions by Applying
The Profit-Taker Model for Hedging

How important a consideration is commission in a hedge situation?

In hedging of securities, brokers will often assert that the small investor cannot participate as successfully because commissions at the retail level can quickly eat up the profits. Perhaps, a more cynical viewpoint is that the person on the street is deliberately discouraged from the more profitable and risk-free situations, as they are reserved for the inner circle of investment dealers. However, it has been my experience that the more progressive and curious brokers are greatly interested in pursuing the Profit-Taker hedge situations for individual clients who have taken the time to make their own decisions. But alas, if the broker is not familiar with the strategy, a knowledgeable customer interested in a Profit-Taker hedge, may find that such a broker will attempt to dissuade the small investor rather than make an effort to understand the hedge.

However, a conscientious broker with one of North America's largest investment houses confessed to me that during a severe recession he considered changing careers because he found it too painful to advise clients of their losses.

He happened to read my book, <u>The Profit-Taker: The Proven Rapid Moneymaker in Good and Bad Markets</u>, and it convinced him that he could be of real service to his clients by making money in bad markets, and in good ones. It is my sincere belief that brokers who care about their clients' money in the same manner as they care about their own, will encourage hedge positions, and will also benefit in the long run by having loyal customers.

You will see in the Profit-Taker case study in Book III, there are large commission savings when using hedge techniques. For example, when you wind up a profitable Profit-Taker Plan, there are no commissions at all!

How should I go about picking a broker representative?

1. Regardless of the field of investment you select, and in which you now will apply the Profit-Taker Rules, do not search for a broker or representative to predict the direction in which the market is going to move. Although it may be fun, there is ample evidence that attempting to out-guess the movement of markets by amateurs or by "professionals" is equally and ultimately unreliable. Most predictions are based on "rear-view mirror" images of the market. The market,

however, has no memory. In my experience, it is the experienced and progressive broker who realizes the futility and unprofitability of predicting the market, who is most open to the Profit-Taker strategies. Remember, you are in control of your own investments when you use the Profit-Taker Rules.

2. Satisfy yourself that your broker is knowledgeable about the implementation of your proposed hedge strategy; do not assume that brokers or the respective representatives are familiar with hedging techniques, such as the Profit-Taker Hedge. Most brokers have had very little formal training in hedge techniques. Don't forget, the broker is not your partner, they just collect their commissions when you buy and when you sell, regardless of whether you win or lose. So persist, and control your own account.

3. Let your broker know that you expect prompt service. Not only should your initial orders be submitted immediately by your representative, but you should be telephoned as soon as the order has been confirmed.

4. Before you make a final selection of an investment representative, visit more than one. Try to visit at least three. This will give you a base for comparisons.

5. Ask to meet the office sales manager of

the investment house, and explain your interest. Request a representative who is knowledgeable about hedging.

6. Consider working with two investment houses. If your initial investment is modest (for example $2,000 - $10,000) you should probably employ only one broker. Once your account is larger, however, make use of two. There is nothing underhanded about this. If you find that one is out of line, it will become apparent sooner. Furthermore, it is good business to let representatives know they are in competition.

Specific comments on commissions are made in Book II and Book III.

As with many things in life, brokers and investment representatives are not perfect. But keep looking for the best, because there is a vast difference between investment houses, as well as between representatives within these houses. It will pay handsome dividends to apply these guidelines.

So in order to receive the best value for your commissions:

Rule 5 is:
Be creative, reduce commissions.

Chapter 8
Big Money in Hedging?
Actual Examples of When the Stock Moves Up, Down and Sideways, and the Results of a Half Hedge Portfolio

The hedge examples in this chapter were submitted by eminent brokers of established investment firms. In the case of the portfolio results (Example 4), the registered broker is the President of a corporation that specializes in half-hedge investment programs. All are truly expert in the skills of applying hedge techniques.

It is very satisfying for me to reveal the results of hedging situations in which the stock moves up, the stock moves down, the stock moves sideways, and in which there is a portfolio of diversified securities. It should not be construed from these examples that it is more advantageous if the stock moves in one direction rather than another.

If you have questions on the details of how such hedges were planned and executed, please refer to Book III, "The Profit-Taker Personal Seminar", which should answer most of your questions about the specifics of setting up such strategies. The sources of each example, that is, the broker and the respective investment firm, are available upon request.

EXAMPLE 1

THE STOCK TREND IS UPWARDS; ANNUALIZED RETURN OF 40.8%

FEDERAL NATIONAL MORTGAGE
4-3/8% OF 1996
(DETAILS FOLLOW)

Example 1: The Stock Trend is Upwards
Federal National Mortgage 4-3.8% of 1996

The Starting Point

Bought	20 bonds at	$895	= $17,900.00
Sold Short	510 shares at	$16-1/4	= $ 8,287.50

Orders Filled on Fluctuation

Bought	170 shares at	$11-3/8
Sold Short	170 shares at	$16-1/4
Sold Short	170 shares at	$20
Sold Short	170 shares at	$24
Sold Short	169 shares at	$28
Bought	170 shares at	$24
Sold Short	169 shares at	$28

Final Order Filled
Converted the bonds and delivered the stock against the short position.

Total Bond Cost	$17,900
Total Cash from Stock	$21,980
Profit:	$ 4,080

Margin required was approximately $5000

Duration : 2 years (81.6% return)

ANNUALIZED RETURN: 40.8%
Author's Note: Commissions not included
Source: Available upon request

67

EXAMPLE 2

THE STOCK TREND IS DOWNWARDS: ANNUALIZED RETURN OF 187.1%

IVACO/DOFASCO CONVERTIBLE
FULL HEDGE
(DETAILS FOLLOW)

Example 2: The Stock Fund is Downwards
Ivaco/Dofasco Convertible Full Hedge

Using the Ivaco Exchangeable Second Preferred

1 Preferred = 1 Dofasco Common
Redeemable   April 1990 @ $33-1/2

Preferred Dividend: $2.72
Payable   15 April, July, Oct., Jan.

Common   Dividend: $1.00
Payable   1 Jan., April, July, Oct.

Opening Position (includes commissions)

Preferred Bought   Common Sold Short
   4000 shares   4000 shares

Total: $146,540.00   Total: $127,901.73

     Difference: $18,638.27 (Initial Investment)
     Debit Spread: $4-3/8 per share

Closing Position (includes commissions)

Preferred Sold   Common Covered
  4000 shares   4000 shares

Total: $125,083.00   Total: $97,990.00

     Difference: $27,093.00
     Credit Spread: $7-1/4 per share

69

Gross Profit: $8,454.73

Dividends

Received:	$2,720.00
Paid Out:	$1,000.00

Net Dividends: $1,720.00

Rental Fees
Charged: $ 328.73
  (Short Sale)

Net Profit: $9,846.00 or 52.8%

Duration: 103 days

ANNUALIZED RETURN: 187.1%

Source: Available upon request

EXAMPLE 3

THE STOCK TREND IS SIDEWAYS:
ANNUALIZED RETURN OF 75%

REPUBLIC AIRLINES
10-1/8% OF 2007
(DETAILS FOLLOW)

Example 3: The Stock Trend is Sideways
Republic Airlines 10-1/8% of 2007

The Starting Point

Bought	15 bonds at	$585.00
Sold Short	500 shares at	$4-1/4

Orders Filled on Fluctuations (Final Order)

Bought	500 shares at	$4-1/2
Sold	15 bonds at	$ 677.50
Loss on shares		-$ 125.00
Gain on bonds		$1,387.50
	Net Gain:	$1,262.50

Margin required: $2,500.00

Duration: 8 months (50.5% return)

ANNUALIZED RETURN: 75%

Author's Note: Commissions not included. Here the "disgruntled" stocks weren't moving much in either direction - but the convertible bonds moved up. So the client took the money and ran. There are so many ways to profit with hedging.

Source: Available upon request

EXAMPLE 4

A PORTFOLIO OF SECURITIES:

PORTFOLIO 1:
ANNUALIZED RETURN OF 91%

PORTFOLIO 2:
ANNUALIZED RETURN OF 75%

HALF HEDGE INVESTMENT PROGRAM
(SEE FOLLOWING LETTER)

Example 4: A Portfolio of Securities

Mr. Don Abrams
(Personal Address)

Dear Don:

I would like to take some of your precious time to bring you up to date on my "Half Hedge Investment Program".

After a three year research program representing approximately seven thousand (7000) hours and a fifty thousand ($50,000) investment, my "Half Hedge Investment Program" was finally launched in 1990. I presently have accumulated some fifteen thousand (15,000) hours of research and application.

During the period of 1991 - 1993 (thirty months).

The DOW JONES INDUSTRIAL AVERAGE increased by 21.79%, or **8.72% per year**.

My "HALF HEDGE INVESTMENT PROGRAM" increased by 74.79%, or **29.92 % per year**.

The average holding period per "Investment position" was three hundred and forty (340) days.

Some four hundred (400) trades were executed during the period, resulting in an average 3.33 trades per week.

No losses were incurred on any trades during the period. This includes the transition period from theory to practical.

The "no losses" phenomenon is due primarily to the screening process which includes around one hundred (100) selection criteria.

The estimated market value at the end of the period was six (6) million dollars.

I presently have a second "Investment Program" in "American and Canadian Corporate Convertible Bonds".

Best Regards,

(Registered Broker)

AUTHOR'S NOTE: The annualized return of 29.2% is based on cash transactions. Conservatively, this return may be at least doubled if margin is utilized.

Source: Available upon request

THE BOTTOM LINE

THE PROFIT-TAKER HEDGE RULES

Rule 1:   Don't waste your time and money trying to predict the direction of the market. (Chapters 2 and 3)

Rule 2:   Plan to profit from small fluctuations. (Chapter 4)

Rule 3:   Use leverage to your advantage. (Chapter 5)

Rule 4:   Use volatility (price action) to condense time. (Chapter 6)

Rule 5:   Be creative, reduce commissions. (Chapter 7)

BOOK II

THE PROFIT-TAKER HEDGE APPLIED TO OTHER INVESTMENTS

Chapter 1
Silver Coins

Rule 1:
Don't waste your time and money trying to predict the direction of the market. (Bk. I, Ch. 2 and 3)

The "stress-free" diversification of the silver coin stems from the knowledge that there is a profit on the upside if there is an increase in the price of silver bullion or in the numismatic value of the coin. And of course you have the assurance that there is a "floor", or a limit, to your loss, as represented by the face value of the coin, for it is this face value of the coins that provides the theoretical floor price below which the value of the coin cannot fall. However, the actual value may be somewhere above that. For instance, if you purchased a bag of silver coins with a face value of $1,000 the theoretical floor would, of course, be $1000. The actual value may be much higher however.

If the actual price of the silver bullion is close to the theoretical floor of $1,000 this situation provides an incentive for many people to buy, but for few to sell, thereby keeping the actual price (or premium) above the theoretical floor (face value).

We can be reassured by history. On

October 27, 1971 the price of silver bullion dropped to $1.298 per ounce. At that price, the silver content of a bag of coins with a face value of $1,000 was worth $934.56; however, the actual price of a bag was $1,129 or with a premium of 12.9 percent above the face value. This was because there was little risk in holding coins when the price could only drop $129 lower.

The floor makes it possible to set an absolute limit to your losses. However, the further the price gets away from the face value, the less useful the floor price becomes. That's why, generally speaking, gold bullion coins with only a relatively small face value, but a high actual value, make a poor vehicle for the Profit-Taker Hedge.

Rule 2:
Plan to profit from small fluctuations. (Bk. I, Ch. 4)

A key factor in setting up the plan to profit from relatively small fluctuations is the "current premium". In the case of silver coin, the premium is the difference between the actual price of the coin and the face value of the coin. Generally speaking, the lower the premium, the more attractive the situation is for a Profit-Taker Hedge.

Establishing the plan to profit from small

fluctuations is as simple and as basic as setting up a plan for "stocks and bonds". Remember to use the face value of the coin as the long-term goal on the downside. The purpose of the plan then is to buy more coins as the premium narrows on the downside and sell them as the premium widens on the upside. This then allows you to profit on the multitude of possible fluctuations between your sub-goals.

A thorough understanding of the Profit-Taker Hedge plan renders planning a silver coin strategy a very simple matter. (See Chapter 4 of Book I and Lesson 10 of Book III)

Let's use the following situations as an example for setting up a Profit-Taker plan for silver coins:

* A 60% premium on the actual price of the Olympic silver coin above the face value.
* The face value of the coin is $10.00.
* Therefore, the actual price of the silver is $16.00.

Now be prepared to taste the excitement of the Profit-Taker:

* Buy 100 silver coins, a total of $1,600.00
* SET THE LONG-TERM GOAL AT 60% OF PURCHASE PRICE, i.e.,

81

divide long-term goals into three equal parts (see following plan).

Your Profit-Taker Plan is simple to set up.

UNIT PRICE		TOTAL
$25.60 LONG-TERM GOAL	(UPSIDE)	$2,560.00
$22.40 SUB-GOAL 2	(UPSIDE)	$2,240.00
$19.20 SUB-GOAL 1	(UPSIDE)	$1,920.00
$16.00 PURCHASE PRICE		$1,600.00
$14.00 SUB-GOAL 1	(DOWNSIDE)	$1,400.00
$12.00 SUB-GOAL 2	(DOWNSIDE)	$1,200.00
$10.00 LONG-TERM GOAL (Face Value of Silver Coin)	(DOWNSIDE)	$1,000.00

* Remember to buy $200.00 (1/3 of the long-term downside goal) of silver coin at each sub-goal downside.
* Remember to sell $320.00 (1/3 of long-term upside goal) on the upside.

Following this plan you will profit with each fluctuation between any two sub-goals regardless of the direction of the market. Remember that coins may prove to be an excellent hedge, but until a profit is taken, they are a non-productive investment, devoid of interest and dividends.

Rule 3:
Use leverage to your advantage. (Bk. I, Ch. 5)

Investments in coins, with a high-percentage bullion value, have by far the most clear-cut argument for magnifying the money working for you. An investor can simply use a physical coin collection for financing a new endeavour. For example, such investors can arrange with a financial institution to hold their silver or gold coin as collateral. This would be considered more secure than a house or car, especially as coins not only have a current value based on the bullion content and -- possibly -- numismatic value; they are also protected by the set face value. Paper securities, such as stocks and bonds can, in theory, be reduced to zero, while if the actual face value of silver coins becomes worthless, the government, in effect, has collapsed.

Rule 4:
Use volatility (price action) to condense time. (Bk. I, Ch. 6)

The price action of silver coins over a period of years has been extremely volatile. The investment house of Solomon Brothers did a survey in June 1985, and found that amongst all investments over the last fifteen years, coins have ranked second in upward volatility and have been outranked only by oil. Today, some investment advisors are putting about five percent of their clients' money into coins.

Rule 5:
Be creative, reduce commissions. (Bk. I, Ch. 7)

Since there is no set market, such as Wall Street, coins are generally an unregulated business. Therefore, the dealers you select are important, as they will post a buy and a sell price. The spread or hedge between the buy and sell price is the dealer's profit. Consequently, there are no commissions. It is a business that can be very profitable, but one must take time to become knowledgeable.

It is also interesting to note that coin collections are not normally taxed at borders, therefore, if one wanted to be creative and travel to different parts of the world that still use silver in their coins, bargains may be obtained for hedging purposes.

Forming or joining a coin collecting club can provide a wealth of knowledge about trading expeditiously.

Chapter 2
Copper Pennies

Rule 1:
Don't waste your time and money trying to predict the direction of the market. (Bk. I, Ch. 2 and 3)

Although the United States and Canadian pennies are not a precious metal, it is appropriate to examine them here as an intriguing and potentially profitable hedge. There is a base price at which the copper metal contained in the penny could become more valuable than the face value of one cent. Therefore, in principle, the lowly penny - in quantity - becomes an exciting hedge for the same reasons as silver and gold coins do.

Timing is critical. The period within which immediate profits can be made, when the metal content is worth more than the face value of circulating coins, is short. However, if you are aware of the situation, this time frame may be sufficiently long enough to make a fortune. For example, in the middle and late 1960's a strange speculation developed in modern coins, specifically in the coins of the U.S. and Canada. In 1965, the alloy used to make U.S. silver coins was changed, and no silver was used. Shortly thereafter, Canadian silver content was reduced until it was stopped after 1968. Throughout this period and after, many "collectors" rushed to the banks to "mine" for the silver in rolls of dimes and quarters. Once the "pay dirt" had been removed, the remaining coins were returned to the banks for more coins. Gradually, the coins containing silver dried up. All the public really knew was that the old coins, containing silver, could be sold for 25% and more over the face value. Very often, the buyers of these coins were not speculators, but private smelters who melted the coins illegally, often realizing a profit margin of over 100%, even including transportation, smelting and other factors.

Will the unprized, lowly copper penny be the next vehicle to generate large immediate profits simply for the sorting? Certainly it is worth being a spectator for an immediate cash hedge.

How do you calculate the value of copper? Well, the U.S. copper penny weighs 48 grains and is 95% copper, which is to say, it contains 45.56 grains of copper and 2.5 grains of zinc. One hundred pennies ($1.00) have, therefore, a net weight of 0.651 pounds of pure copper. (Divide $1.00 by 0.65142 = $1.54). Because the penny is a non-precious metal coin, it is based on the avoirdupois system, not the troy.

Therefore, the base price of copper U.S.

pennies is $1.54 avoirdupois pound. When the
quoted price rises above $1.54 per pound, the
U.S. copper penny becomes a candidate for a
hedge strategy. That is, the copper content is
worth more than the face value. Smelting costs
are a consideration.

The current price of copper per pound may
be found readily under the New York Commodity
Exchange in any comprehensive financial paper.

Rule 2:
Plan to profit from small fluctuations. (Bk. I, Ch. 4)

The plan for setting up a Profit-Taker
Hedge with copper pennies would be essentially
the same as setting up the plan as previously
described for silver coins. However, when the
time arrives in which there is a premium charged
over and above the face value of the "red cent",
perhaps you'll be able to buy them at the bank
for the face value. At least, this windfall was the
case for the alert with silver quarters and dimes,
for a few months at least.

Rule 3:
Use leverage to your advantage. (Bk. I, Ch. 5)

No doubt, the leverage will be as attractive
as with the silver coins.

Rule 4:
Use volatility (price action) to condense time (Bk. I, Ch. 6)

The season's price range, as well as the current week's high and low, are given to you under the New York Commodity Exchange. To calculate the volatility (price action) for purposes of comparison, simply subtract the low price from the high and divide by the current price (times 100 for percentage).

Rule 5:
Be creative, reduce commissions. (Bk. I, Ch. 7)

In the case of copper pennies, as yet there is no market to attract traders, consequently, there are no commissions on "buy" and "sell" spreads.

Chapter 3
A Real Estate Hedge

Rent With a Lease

Rule 1:
Don't waste your time and money trying to predict the direction of the market. (Bk. I, Ch. 2 and 3)

Most people who rent would prefer to own, but can't afford the down payment required, or feel uncomfortable with it.

In a rising real estate market, they would like to share in the touted equity gains one hears so much about. It is a major hurdle. Renters often get caught on the hamster wheel. Renters who want to buy a home of their own will begin to save for the down payment. However, by the time they save what they originally thought was sufficient, the price of real estate will have often vaulted again. They are caught in a vicious circle.

Predicting the real estate market can be as treacherous as predicting the stock market. The big difference is that it is easier for the owner of a home to fantasize about the value at any given time, whereas the stock or bond holder knows that the value of their securities is based on the last daily sale. It is also more likely that the home owner will ride the fluctuations of the real estate market, hoping that when the time comes to sell, it will have peaked. A difficult feat indeed to accomplish!

Is there a true hedge in real estate for the renter? Can the Profit-Taker mind-set be applied by the small real estate investor? One such relatively unknown hedge is renting with an option to buy. This is a very creative area of investing, and there are many variations of the theme. For example, a home owner may feel the fair market value of his house is $150,000. However, there are no takers within the time frame he has allowed himself. Enter the renter interested in eventually owning his own home. For the privilege of "buying" the home, a price of $160,000 may be set now at the option of the renter buying in two or three years.

Here the renter is setting up a hedge. In the next two or three years, the equity in the home may increase over the fair market price set in the original option, obviously to the renter's advantage. The accumulated "rent" as well as the renter's share of the increased equity, may more than offset the down payment of the house.

A renter who has the option to buy also has time to become familiar with the neighborhood before he makes the final decision;

he can get to know all about the house, transportation facilities, schools, and so on. This hedge creates a more flexible situation for the "renter" and allows him more time to consolidate, and even save to purchase a home.

Why should the renter ever be given such a "break"? A primary reason is to allow the owner time to obtain the full market value of the house. Renting with an option to buy may allow a higher rent, which can be used to pay off a mortgage on a new home. For example, there are many such "emergency" type situations, such as a rather sudden new job offer that requires a transfer to another city.

The owner may receive a cash payment, for example $2,000, for the option to buy. Of course, this "deposit" would be forfeited if the renter decided not to buy.

The renter who has an option to buy is likely to be imbued with a pride of ownership. After all, the renter may be the next owner of the home and, is thus a resident property manager. Owner-occupied properties tend to increase in value more quickly than rented properties. Therefore, the owner is more likely to obtain the specific value he believes it to be worth.

There are many variations on the theme of renting with the option to buy. Some real estate firms have developed or may be encouraged to offer a service whereby they attempt to match up the renters or "occupants" (as they've named them) and the investors. This motivation is similar, in principle, to the "renting with an option to buy", but there is a difference. Like "renting with an option to buy", the potential home buyer or occupant, doesn't require a down payment. The investor provides the down payment and covers the legal fees involved in buying the house. The occupant pays the mortgage and any costs, such as heat and hydro, associated with running the house. Until such time as the arrangement is complete and the investor is paid back, the house is co-owned by the investor and the occupant.

At the end of the three to five year period, the occupant and the investor split the hoped-for capital appreciation of the property. Unlike the renter with an option to buy, the occupant is obliged to take out a new mortgage, and he pays the investor the down payment and any legal fees that were incurred.

However, in this arrangement, the investor also is in a true hedge situation. The investors can double their money on the downside in as short a time as five years, and on the upside, in as little as four. For example, at current rates, the return in the investment can be about eighteen percent per year, ninety percent over five years if a property valued at

$100,000 appreciates at six percent per year for five years. It may be reassuring to the investor if the occupant may, at anytime after the third year, purchase the investor's fifty percent interest. However, the occupant may agree that in no event shall the purchase price be less than an amount that reflects a minimum of six percent average annual increase. It must not be forgotten that the investor's risk is reduced by diversifying in several properties.

In both cases, the renter with an option to buy or the occupant with an option to buy may assume sole ownership of the home at the end of a pre-set period.

Rule 2:
Plan to profit from small fluctuations. (Bk. I, Ch. 4)

The renter with an option to buy may well profit from price fluctuations, although the locked-in gains may be over a longer term than in the case with convertible bonds, for example. The time frame would be more like two to three years; however, the profits can be very substantial indeed.

How the plan is set up depends largely on the specific arrangements of the lease with an option to buy. But what could be more disciplined than paying a monthly rent which might result in the ownership of the home.

Rule 3:
Use leverage to your advantage. (Bk., Ch. 5)

Perhaps the most basic bonus that renters with an option to buy have is the fact that as future home buyers, they are able to use the investor or landlord as a source of risk-free leverage on the down payment. Now, with little or no capital investment, the renter with an option to buy may participate in local real estate appreciation.

On the side of the "landlords", one sees that their money may be invested for a period of time of over two years, but they will less likely suffer from "owner-tenant syndrome" as the potential owner will live on the property. For example, the landlord may have an arrangement whereby the renter with an option to buy does the painting and any renovations needed on the property. In effect, the landlord simply puts up the money and enjoys the increased cash flow (rent), secure in the knowledge that he has not received less than the asking price.

The landlord is thus providing the incentive for the renter to purchase the home. For now, the renter has a sense of ownership, because the rent may be used as "equity" and be applied to the down payment.

Rule 4:
Use volatility (price action) to condense time. (Bk. I, Ch. 6)

Obviously, the renter with an option to buy will gain a larger share of the profits if the volatility of the property is in a strong upward market.

Rule 5:
Be creative, reduce commissions. (Bk. I, Ch. 7)

There is no real estate commission to encumber the fair market price if the "rental-manager" exercises the option to buy.

Real estate agents may also benefit from being an investment match-maker. The company may charge a fee to both the investor and the occupant. Investors are often charged about two percent of the purchase of the real estate; occupants are often charged a set amount, for example, seven hundred dollars.

Chapter 4
Bank Passbook Hedging

Rule 1:
Don't waste your time and money trying to predict the direction of the market. (Bk. I, Ch. 2 and 3)

Spreads between U.S. and Canadian currencies are often so beguiling and so accessible that they are a natural for application of the principles of the Profit-Taker technique. "Bank passbook hedging" is also a way by which the knowledgeable person can jump in with both feet, profiting regardless of the direction of the economy. For example, when Canadian banks were paying 9-1/2 percent to 10 percent on day-to-day savings accounts, while U.S. banks were paying 5-1/2 percent to 6 percent on the same, the incentive to move U.S. dollars to greener pastures becomes almost irresistible. It is stressed that such opportunities are not exceptional. But hold on! Interest rates are only part of the story.

Small U.S. and Canadian hedgers can interplay the U.S. and Canadian dollar in almost the same way as the professionals. Almost every American or Canadian who makes a profit on the foreign currency exchange makes it inadvertently if the currency trend runs in the right direction. By applying the Profit-Taker technique, the small investor can take a great deal of the risk out of predicting, and profit from the fluctuations. For example, the small investor does not have to invest in Canadian dollars at a whopping big discount and pray that the U.S. currency will hold steady or go down in price. However, there is that omnipresent danger that the forces behind the Canadian discount -- political infighting, inflation, big discount deficits, and threats of Quebec's separation -- will continue unresolved and drive the Canadian dollar further into a nose-dive.

Opportunities when $1,000 U.S. buys something like $1,150 Canadian dollars, depending on where you shop, and commands 5 percent more interest over what the equivalent dollar might fetch in a U.S. day-to-day savings account are no longer rare. Apparently, Canadian banks are also more than anxious to do business in the U.S. by mail, and certainly the reverse is true.

Tom Pullen was formerly at the helm of a Canadian edition of a U.S. bank since its inception. According to Pullen, "people use our banks as a holding tank for their U.S. dollar accounts". He quickly adds that U.S. banks are not in Canada to compete with Canadian banks, but to offer convenient American banking for Canadians. Such banks located in both countries are Citi Bank, Barclays Bank, Amex

Bank, Chase Manhattan Bank and Bank of America

For example, the bank passbook hedgers have U.S. and Canadian bank accounts, and when the Canadian dollar goes up, the players win because they profit from the gains it has made. Now they can buy more U.S. dollars. Also, if the market trend is upwards, they are collecting favorable interest rates on the Canadian dollar while watching the value of the "stock" rise.

Conversely, if the Canadian market goes down, they often collect even higher interest rates on the Canadian dollar but have the added bonus of being able to buy more Canadian dollars cheaper from the funds in the U.S. account, thereby having more money on which to collect the interest. Either way, the participants have ideal potential for profit.

Of course, the bank passbook hedge is not limited to only U.S. and Canadian currencies; it can also be used between other foreign currencies, for example, between Canadian dollars and U.K. pounds, or between Canadian dollars and Japanese yen, benefiting from the differences in the current interest rates between the selected countries. (Figure 1)

Tom Pullen told me of a "number of

Canadians who, in their own subtle way, are hedging against the Canadian dollar and are saying 'I need the money in the U.S. at some point, because I am going to retire there or have my pension money which I've destined to the U.S.', so whether they like it or not, they are hedging". "Furthermore", Pullen adds that "we have officers in the bank who are doing that."

Rule 2:
Plan to profit from small fluctuations. (Bk. I, Ch. 4)

It is critical to make the actual executions at predetermined sub-goals. Nothing is gained by merely watching the fluctuations occur and experiencing the emotions of one day being "up" and the next day being "down", much like a romance. So set up the Profit-Taker plan in much the same manner as described Book III, Lesson 10, using convertible bonds. Follow the same steps. If, for example, you were hedging U.S. dollars day-to-day against Canadian, you would always convert U.S. dollars to Canadian dollars at the present sub-goals on the downside and convert Canadian funds to U.S. on the upside. If planned properly, each fluctuation

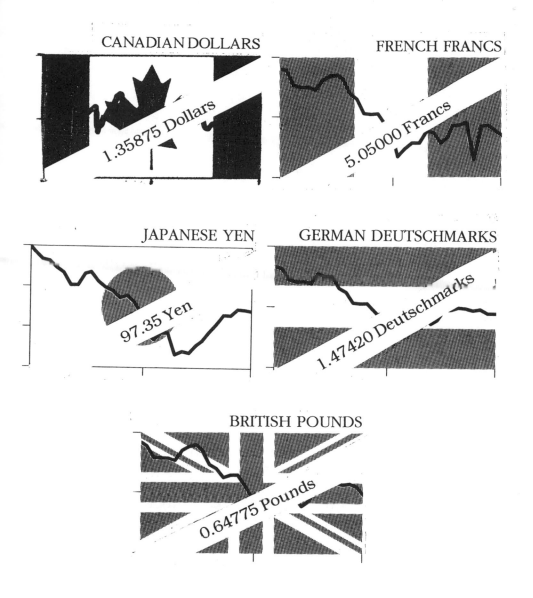

Figure 1. What One United States Dollar Buys in Other Currency
(to August 19, 1995)

would produce a profit regardless of the direction of the market.

When setting the long term goal on the downside, be certain it is a goal below which you believe the dollar will not fall. For example, you might establish the long-term goal on the downside at the ultraconservative point of "0". Then sub-divide into perhaps three equal parts. However, if the movement of the dollar is not sufficiently volatile to lock-in profits between your sub-goals, you may wish to set it at a low point you consider as conservative.

Tom Pullen agrees that attempting to predict the direction of the market is a waste of time. But he, too, points out that it is not sufficient simply to watch the value of your U.S. or Canadian funds fluctuate, you must take action. Pullen points out that "both stocks and interest rates are affected by different things... innuendos, implications, statements of fact, stupidity, and statements by people in very strong positions... Play the fluctuations and actually take your profits. The problem is whether people will take their profits... If you set your criteria and then don't follow them, it's like having your bible but never reading it. You've got to have a system and the discipline to follow it... A lot of people we're dealing with may make money, but they make it because of circumstances, not because of design. And if they look back on it, maybe they would have made more money had they played it by design."

When interest rates are higher in Canada, compared with the U.S., there is an additional protection on the downside of the Canadian dollar. For example, Canadian Treasury bills have offered yields that are four to five percentage points higher than the equivalent U.S. debt issues. When a currency like the Canadian dollar reaches near record lows, there is potential for double-barreled profits.

Rule 3:
Use leverage to your advantage. (Bk. I, Ch. 5)

With such conservative investments as Canadian and U.S. T-bills, it will not be difficult to obtain attractive leverage. Conversely, the lure of speculative future contracts on financial securities with their leverage of four to five percent margin on the dollar may be very tempting. However, remember that these options are contracts only, and when they expire, they are, quite literally, not worth the paper they are printed on. Furthermore, they do not bear interest.

Rule 4:
Use volatility (price action) to condense time.

(Bk. I, Ch. 6)

Use the volatility of the money markets to your advantage. Typically, a 20 percent to 30 percent margin would be considered by many to be conservative. As has been referred to in the example of Rule 3, that if the Canadian dollar performs poorly, then the Canadian or American investor transfers more of the U.S. funds in his Profit-Taker plan to buy Canadian dollars for greater profits, with the confidence that the Canadian dollar is unlikely to collapse. Even if it did, we would all have more to worry about than profits in the bank. Also, volatility will not affect term or T-bill deposits, as these are guaranteed by the issuing institutions. An example of this occurred in the recession-burdened early eighties, when people were buying savings bonds that matured five years later at 20 percent a year compounded.

Rule 5:
Be creative, reduce commissions. (Bk. I, Ch. 7)

Remember, there is a "buy-sell" ratio. A dollar that trades at 80 cents today and you turn around and sell it tomorrow with the price still at 80 cents, you would not receive 80 cents. There is a built-in cost of three to four cents on every dollar. Tom Pullen cautions the investor "not to play the game in a tight ratio. You have to see at least a five or six cent level to make a profit. This spread is like a commission. Sometimes a fee or commission is charged, but shop around. It is not always the case". Tom Pullen assures the small investor that the same principles apply to the small investor as to the large investor. When I asked him the approximate minimum amount that he would be interested in for an individual, he replied: "We deal with people with $50.00 in their savings account. Our service charges are minimal or non-existent, depending on the balance in your account." This is not the case with many Canadian banks.

Your U.S. funds are always safe and secure and protected when deposited in a bank like Citi Bank. For example, at no cost to you, your deposit is protected up to $100,000 by the U.S. Federal Deposit Insurance Corporation.

There are no U.S. withholding laws, and no regulatory reporting requirements for non-residents. (This does not, of course, lessen a U.S. or Canadian taxpayer's obligation to report interest earned).

Chapter 5
The Closed-End Mutual Fund Hedge

Rule 1:
Don't waste your time and money trying to predict the direction of the market. (Bk. I, Ch. 2 and 3)

Closed-end funds are a different breed of investment than mutual funds. Do not confuse these! Closed-end funds are more attractive and adaptable to hedging. Closed-end funds are usually issued in the same manner as stocks traded on a listed exchange or over the counter. Mutual fund units do not trade on the public exchange like stocks and bonds, you simply buy units from representatives of the mutual fund management company. As a result, the mutual fund expands or shrinks based on investor demand. In effect, the price of a mutual fund is always based on its Net Asset Value (NAV). "No load" mutual funds are sold at their NAV. Load funds are sold at their NAV plus a sales charge. Mutual funds are redeemed at NAV when an investor wishes to sell.

It is important to note that for hedging purposes, unlike that of open-end funds, the value of closed-end fund units is not determined solely by the net asset value; how investors "feel" about the closed-end fund, for whatever reason, also has a direct effect on the trading value of the closed-end fund stock. Consequently, prices of closed-end funds nearly always diverge from their net asset values, occasionally commanding a "premium" that is higher than their net asset value, <u>but often they trade below their underlying value or at a "discount"</u>.

U.S. and Canadian closed-end funds often trade at big discounts relative to their net asset values. The discounts vary greatly. Recently, it was not uncommon to see several closed-end funds in the 30 percent discount range, with one listed at 41 percent. Furthermore, dividends are paid one hundred cents on the net asset value, even though you bought it at a discount.

There are a number of reasons why this discount develops in closed-end mutual funds. The chief reason is that the closed-end funds are simply not as profitable to the investment house. Again, it is important here that you, the individual investor, do your homework. In most firms, the registered representative is encouraged to sell the company's research recommendations. If these are the open-end mutual funds, then the representative complies, especially if the commission is doubled. However, remember that if you purchase a $10.00 share of an open-end fund, the price is based on the net asset value of the fund PLUS usually an approximately 8 percent commission, for a total of $10.80. If you purchase a closed-end fund with an equivalent $10.00 net asset value, besides getting the share at a discount from the net asset value, for example, at \$8.00 or \$9.00 a share, you only pay the commission customarily paid for other listed shares, possibly one quarter or less of the open-end mutual fund commission.

The domino theory may also apply here. Sometimes, investors concentrate on funds with substantial discounts, thereby causing the other closed-end funds to gravitate to discounts. The principle of supply and demand is still at work!

It should be noted that operating costs of the closed-end funds are deducted from the yield of that fund, possibly forcing a discount.

Now we are about to set up our plan to profit on the fluctuations, regardless of whether the trend is up or down. The advantage of employing the closed-end mutual fund, rather than just a volatile stock, is that the closed-end fund is comprised of many stocks and therefore it is highly unlikely that the entire fund will fall to zero (that is, bankruptcy). The exception to this is when the fund is highly leveraged. This can be ascertained in advance by researching information based on the charter of the fund. The fact that the fund is highly diversified amongst a number of stocks is an important advantage when setting up a Profit-Taker hedge, as it is assuring when the fund will continue to fluctuate between the sub-goals without going to zero. The two important advantages are that, one, you start with a hefty discount and, two, for practical purposes your investment will not go bankrupt, therefore, it will continue to produce profitable fluctuations until you plan is completed. We now understand why we are prepared to set up a Profit-Taker plan using a closed-end mutual fund, rather than simply turning to a stock.

Rule 2:
Plan to profit from small fluctuations. (Bk. I, Ch. 4)

At this point, I would like to introduce you to a Miami broker who has truly distinguished himself in the specialized area of closed-end mutual funds, not only in the U.S., but in Canada and the U.K., as well. His advisory firm manages money for mostly large institutions and then subsequently his brokerage firm executes the orders into closed-end mutual funds. Both firms bear his name - Thomas Herzfeld. He is a very busy man! As well as managing these closed-end fund investments, he publishes the Encyclopedia of the Closed-End Fund Industry, as well as writing a definitive monthly research report. In addition, he writes six articles a year for Barron's. After accumulating such knowledge about closed-end mutual funds, what technique does this man utilize to take advantage of the opportunity these funds offer?

Listen to this. Recently, I asked him: "What would you think of a strategy - a very straightforward strategy - of buying as the discounts opens or increases, and selling as it closes. It's a type of averaging down, only based on the discount (fluctuations), without short selling it?" He replied simply: "That's primarily what we do. That's my main business."

As Mr. Herzfeld indicates here, the characteristics of closed-end mutual funds are most appropriate for hedging purposes.

You can apply the Profit-Taker Plan using the closed-end mutual fund, thereby allowing you to profit from relative small fluctuations in their price. (It is most important that you understand how the specifics of the Profit-Taker Plan are executed as explained in Book III: The Personal Seminar Section). For example, you have selected a volatile closed-end fund with a 50 percent discount; that is, the Net Asset Value per unit is currently $60.00, and the Market Value or Purchase Price is $30.00. You might set up your plan as follows:

- a. double your purchase price to obtain the long-term goal (upside)
- b. divide into three equal parts on the upside and the downside
- c. no short sale is used in this hedge

$60	Long-Term Goal	(Uptrend)
$50	Subgoal 2	(Uptrend)
$40	Subgoal 1	(Uptrend)
$30	Purchase Price	
$20	Subgoal 1	(Downtrend)
$10	Subgoal 2	(Downtrend)
$ 0	Long-Term Goal	(Downtrend)

<u>REMEMBER:</u>

1. the discount tends to widen on the downside, creating further resistance on the downside;

2. the discount tends to close on the upside, increasing the volatility of the fund;

3. as a closed-end fund represents many stocks, it is highly unlikely to go to zero on the downside;

4. always buy at the point of your sub-goals on the downside, and sell at the point of your sub-goals on the upside.

As with the convertible Profit-Taker Hedge, used as an example in the Personal Seminar Section, you profit on fluctuations, regardless of whether the trend is up or down.

<u>Rule 3:</u>
Use leverage to your advantage. (Bk. I, Ch. 4)

Leverage has a unique advantage when closed-end funds are used for hedging, such as in this Profit-Taker Hedge. Usually, when an

111

investor buys a round lot of 100 shares for $60.00, for a total of $6,000.00, the maximum margin provided by the broker would be 50 percent or $3,000.00. For this privilege, interest would be charged.

Based on our previous example, the same investor could purchase a round lot of a closed-end fund with a Net Asset Value of $60.00, for the purchase price of $30.00 (Market Price), for a total of $3,000.00, or 50 percent discount. Not only would he not pay any interest on the difference, but he would collect the dividends on the entire amount of the Net Asset Value of $6,000.00.

Rule 4:
Use volatility (price action) to condense time. (Bk. I, Ch. 6)

As with other investments used for the Profit-Taker Hedge, welcome all the price action you can find. The same rules apply to the closed-end fund for determining volatility as apply to convertibles in the Personal Seminar Section (Book III). When selecting closed-end funds with deep discounts, you create a situation with greater volatility than if you owned the actual stock the fund is comprised of - particularly on the uptrend. Remember, the more fluctuation between your sub-goals, the more profit you make.

Rule 5:
Be creative, reduce commissions. (Bk. I, Ch. 7)

As with any common stocks, commissions vary widely, depending on a number of factors. Therefore, it is important that you determine your commission costs in advance and adjust your hedge plan accordingly. Realize that with the Profit-Taker Hedge using a closed-end mutual fund, you are paying commissions only on the long position, as there is no 'short-selling' involved here when setting up your plan.

BOOK III

THE PROFIT-TAKER PERSONAL SEMINAR
OR
AN IN-DEPTH EXAMPLE OF HOW THE
PROFIT-TAKER HEDGE IS APPLIED TO
STOCKS AND BONDS

Lesson 1
The Introduction

This is a crash course on the stock market, starting with the basics and progressing very rapidly. If you are familiar with the ABC's of stocks and bonds, then skim this part as a review. I simply do not want to exclude anything that might prevent you from appreciating the full excitement of the Profit-Taker concept. First, we will take a fast trip through a financial newspaper. The paper I have selected is perhaps the most complete financial paper in North America: <u>Barron's National Business and Financial Weekly (Barron's)</u>. Once you understand this example, you will have no trouble with financial sections of other North American newspapers. You will find that the financial newspapers read very much alike. Running through the index on the inside page of Barron's enables the reader to know the items covered in the issue.

Should you own common stock, you will likely turn to the Stock Exchange Composite List immediately. (Figure 2)

Students sometimes have problems with the abbreviations of corporate names. Don't be overly concerned. Identification becomes easier with practice.

117

NEW YORK STOCK EXCHANGE COMPOSITE LIST

52-Weeks High	Low	Name and Dividend	Sales 100s	Yield Pct.	P/E Ratio	Week's High	Week's Low	Last	Net Chg.	EARNINGS Interim or Fiscal Year	EARNINGS Year ago	DIVIDENDS Latest divs.	DIVIDENDS Record date	DIVIDENDS Payment date
		A-B-C												
37½	26½	AAR .48	992	1.6	18	30⅛	29¼	29½	— ½	Feb9m1.21	1.10	q.12	1-29	3-5
9¾	8½	ACM n 1.01	791	11.1		9¼	9	9⅛				M.084	3-9	3-23
11⅝	10½	ACMIn 1.26	3037	11.7		11	10¾	10¾	— ⅛			M.10½	3-9	3-23
9⅞	7¼	ACM M n1.01	1339	12.4		8¼	8	8⅛				M.084	3-9	3-23
12⅛	11⅜	ACMMM	746			11¾	11½	11⅝	+ ⅛			.114	3-19-90	3-30-90
11½	10	ACM Sc 1.26	5132	12.1		10¾	10⅜	10⅜	— ¼			M.10½	3-30	4-12
9⅜	8⅜	ACMSp 1.01	x2980	11.9		8⅞	8½	8½	— ¼			M.084½	4-6	4-20
22⅝	13	AL Lab .16	628	.7	21	22⅜	21¾	21¾	— ¼	89Dec1.06	.87	q.04	4-12	4-26
4⅛	3⅛	AMCA .12e	108	3.8	39	3¼	3⅛	3⅛		89Dec.08	D.11	.15	12-1-89	12-29-89
6⅛	2⅝	AM Intl	3549		9	3	d 2⅝	2¾	— ⅛	Jan6mD.05	.12	Y		10-30-84
23½	16⅜	AM In pf 2	57	12.0		16⅞	16½	16⅝				q.50	5-1	5-15
107¼	52½	AMR	19759		9	65⅜	63¼	63½	— 1	89Dec7.16	7.92	Y		2-15-80
27	25	ANR pf 2.67	17	10.4		25¾	25¼	25¾	+ ¼			q.66⅞	2-15	3-1
24⅞	23¼	ANR pf2.12										q.53	2-15	3-1
5⅛	3⅛	ARX	213			3¾	3½	3⅝	+ ⅛	Dec6m.11	D.66	Y		5-25-88
72¾	39	ASA 3a	4114	5.8		52½	50	51⅞	— ¼	88DecNil	Nil	q.75	2-16	2-23
70⅜	53¼	AbtLab 1.68	15956	2.5	18	67⅞	65¼	67⅝	+ 1⅞	89Dec3.85	3.33	q.42	4-12	5-15
17¼	11¼	Abitibi g .50	246			13¾	13¼	13⅜	— ⅜	89Decg.70	g2.60	q.12½	4-16	4-30
13	8⅞	AcmeC .40	206	4.1	11	9⅞	9⅝	9¾	+ ⅛	✚ Dec3m.20	.08	q.10	5-4	5-18
9¾	7	AcmeE .32	204	3.8	11	9⅛	8⅜	8⅜	— ⅝	Dec26w.34	.32	q.08	2-7	3-5
38½	28⅛	Acusn	3919		22	36¾	35¼	35⅞	+ ⅜	Sep9m1.16	.82			
16½	13⅛	AdaEx 2.06e	414	13.1		15⅞	15½	15¾	+ ⅛			.12	2-20-90	3-1-90
15⅜	7⅜	Adobe	959			13⅛	12½	12⅝	— ⅝	89DecD1.05	D.17			
20¼	16⅞	Adob pf 1.84	162	9.7		19¼	18¾	19				q.46	4-24	5-15
21⅝	19⅞	Adob pf 2.40	34	11.2		21½	21⅛	21⅜	— ⅛			q.60	4-24	5-15
10½	6⅞	AMD	15768		20	9½	8⅞	8⅞	— ¼	Dec53w.44	.11			
35	28¼	AMD pf 3	14	9.6		32	31¼	31¼				q.75	3-1	3-15
10⅛	5	Advest .16	507	3.1	7	5½	5⅛	5⅛	— ½	Dec3m.12	.08	q.04	2-28	3-15
62½	48⅜	AetnLf 2.76	5988	5.5	9	51	49⅝	50		89Dec5.69	6.13	q.69	4-27	5-15
14	9⅞	AfilPb .24	2588	2.3		10½	10⅛	10⅜	— ⅛	Dec53w.63	.75	q.06	5-14	6-1
25	16⅜	Ahmans .88	11641	5.3	9	17¾	16⅝	16¾	— ¾	89Dec1.95	2.05	q.22	5-8	6-1
3⅞	1⅞	Aileen	263			2	d 1⅞	1⅞	— ⅛	Jan13wD.22	D.18			
53¼	40	AirPrd 1.32	14462	2.6	13	51⅞	50½	50¾	— 1½	Dec3m.90	X1.11	q.33	4-5	5-14
48	22⅞	AirbFrt .60	1169	1.3	18	u48	47⅛	47⅜		89Dec2.67	X1.01	q.15	2-20	3-6
25⅛	15½	Airgas	1160		15	16½	15¾	15⅞	— ⅞	Dec9m.46	.30			
20¾	16⅞	Airlease 2.40	149	13.4	9	18¼	17¾	17⅞		89Dec1.99	2.22	q.60	3-30	5-15
23⅜	21¼	AlaP pf2.08e	200	9.5		22	22	22	— ¼			.47	3-6	4-1
10¼	8⅝	AlaP dpf .87	107	9.2		9⅝	9⅜	9½				q2.18	3-6	4-1
98⅝	88½	AlaP pf 9	z1100	9.7		93¾	93	93	+ ⅜			q2.25	3-6	4-1
107	102	AlaP pf11										q2.75	3-6	4-1
103½	93	AlaP pf 9.44	z2920	9.7		99¼	97	97	— 1			q2.36	3-6	4-1
93	81	AlaP pf 8.16	z150	9.5		88	86	86				q2.04	3-6	4-1
91	82	AlaP pf 8.28	z100	9.5		87½	87½	87½	+ 1½			q2.07	3-6	4-1
30½	19¼	AlskAir .20	1279	.8	9	23¾	23⅜	23¾	+ ⅛	89Dec2.71	2.37	q.05	4-12	5-4
23½	15¾	Albnyln .35	420	2.0	10	17⅜	16⅛	17⅜	+ 1⅛	89Dec1.75	1.46	q.08¾	3-9	4-2
26⅝	16⅜	Alberto s .20	539	.9	20	24	22¾	23½	— ⅛	Dec3m.25	.21			

FIGURE 2.

Headings for Stock Listings

Hi and Lo of the Current Year

In <u>Barron's</u> they use the current year prices of the previous fifty-two week period.

Stocks are listed in eighths of a point. An eighth of a point is an eighth of a dollar or twelve and one-half cents. For example, if the listing is 8-3/4, the value of the stock is $8.75. While if a stock quotation appeared as 5-1/8, it would be worth $5.125.

Dividends means the dividends over the past four quarters. In the example of Airlease (Figure 2) the dividend is $2.40.

Hi and Lo (Weekly or Daily)

These prices are for the previous week or day. In the case of <u>Barron's</u>, since it is a weekly, it gives the Hi and Lo for the week. Most financial newspapers are dailies, so their reports will be for the previous day's Hi and Lo. In the example, Airlease's weekly, Hi was 18-1/4, its Lo was 17-3/4.

Change

If nothing is mentioned, the closes are the same. In the underlined example, there was no change.

This is the difference between the close of the most recent business day (or week) and the previous business day (or week).

Volume

This reflects the number of stocks traded. In most financial newspapers, "volume" or "sales" are quoted in hundreds, so when it states 149 for Airlease under "Sales", it really means the volume of sales is 14,900 shares sold over the period of a week.

In Canada, preferred shares and common stock only are traded on the stock exchange. In the United States, many bonds also are traded on the stock exchange, in a similar way as the common stock. Bonds in Canada are traded 'over-the-counter', that is, over the telephone, between investment houses.

When reading the financial papers, be sure to become familiar with the legend. It varies from financial paper to financial paper and is usually listed at the end of the stock exchange data.

There are approximately two hundred stock exchanges in the world, in some sixty one nations. There are twenty exchanges in North America, the biggest being the New York Stock Exchange. The American Stock Exchange, also called ASE or AMEX is also located in New York. There are five exchanges in Canada. Toronto, Montreal, Winnipeg, Calgary, and Vancouver.

In the financial newspapers, there are always articles about how the exchanges behaved on the previous business day and why. I often find them amusing. Brokers, for instance, are sometimes quoted anonymously. Brokers are always expected to be bullish on the market, and are often asked to comment on why the market went up or down the previous day. For some reason it is thought that if they are quoted anonymously, they will be more likely tell the truth. You are expected to believe them if they are not identified, as this is supposed to allow greater objectivity. They justify past stock moves in many ways. But valid reasons for the trends of the following day are hard to find!

Often there is a sample section from the New York Stock Exchange and the American Stock Exchange in <u>The Globe and Mail</u>. However, whenever possible, you should use an American listing, such as the <u>Barron's</u> or the <u>Wall Street Journal</u> when researching U.S. stocks, because the listings are more complete.

The Indexes (Refer to Figure 3)

The U.S. stock markets have great influence on the Canadian markets. The most common index is the Dow Jones Industrial Average. Sometimes it is argued that this is not the best index; the thirty blue chip industrial stocks that the Dow Jones is based on cannot be representative of the whole market, as they are all very conservative. The Dow Jones has been around since the turn of the century. Only two stocks that were on the original list are still listed. A graph of the Dow Jones (Figure 4), over a period of time, shows that the only thing you can count on in the stock market is that it will fluctuate -- because it always has. And, likewise, it very seldom repeats the same pattern.

It is interesting to note that Black Thursday, October 24, 1929 was not the lowest point on the Dow Chart. That happened three years later, after many strong rallies. At that time, a great many investors got back into the market believing that the worst was over, only to lose more. By the way, this was the day that people, when they checked into hotels, were asked whether the room was to be used for sleeping or jumping.

There are other indexes besides the Dow Jones. The New York Most Active Index indicates the greatest volume, but remember, that doesn't mean the most active price. The

NEW YORK

NEW YORK MARKET STATISTICS

DOW JONES AVERAGES

	Volume	Open	High	Low	Close	Change	52-wk high	52-wk low
30 industrials	16,148,500	2879.46	2901.98	2865.84	2880.69	+1.98	2935.89	2440.06
20 Trn	3,161,500	1143.61	1152.92	1133.39	1142.70	unch	1532.01	1031.83
15 Util	4,638,600	208.50	210.39	207.49	210.01	+1.38	236.23	203.09
65 Stk	23,948,000	1029.90	1038.25	1023.74	1031.07	+1.46	1111.10	942.68

MOST ACTIVE

(based on unrevised figures)

Name	Vol 100s	High	Low	Close	Chg
Motel 6	28819	18	16 1/8	16 3/8	− 1 5/8
AT&T	20157	38 7/8	38 1/2	38 1/2	− 1/8
AmExp	x19914	31 1/8	30 1/2	30 3/4	+ 1/4
PhilMr s	13331	46 3/4	46 1/8	46 1/2	+ 1/8
LA Gr s	12830	30 5/8	29 1/8	30 5/8	+ 1 5/8
Baxter	12432	24 1/2	23 7/8	24	− 3/8
Citicorp	11408	23 1/8	22 1/2	22 5/8	− 1/4
MfrHan	11275	34 1/2	34	34 1/2	—
RJR Nb	wt10653	7	6 1/2	6 7/8	—
BrMySq	x10555	64 1/2	63 1/4	63 3/8	− 1/2
Magntk	10467	11 3/8	10 3/4	11	—
GenEl	10349	69 5/8	69 1/8	69 1/4	—

MARKET BREADTH

	Yesterday	Previous
Issues traded	2006	1993
Advances	954	911
Declines	583	559
Unchanged	469	523
52-week highs	53	62
52-week lows	50	43

Volume advances	75,299,600
Volume declines	49,635,900
Total volume	145,500,000

STANDARD AND POOR'S INDEXES

	High	Low	Close	Change	52-wk high	52-wk low
400 industrials	422.06	419.89	420.51	+0.27	428.24	283.58
20 transportation	276.63	275.20	276.02	+0.45	331.07	251.57
40 finance	28.98	28.85	28.93	+0.06	35.18	26.59
40 utilities	141.40	140.66	141.39	+0.47	157.86	132.27
500 stocks	359.09	357.30	358.02	+0.39	367.40	317.98
100 stocks	341.43	339.60	339.80	−0.44	349.20	294.88

NYSE CLOSING INDEXES

	Composite	Industrials	Transport	Utilities	Financial
Net change	+0.29	+0.23	+0.53	+0.28	+0.35
Close	196.47	242.33	172.56	91.87	144.75

ASSOCIATED PRESS AVERAGES

	Industrials	Rails	Utilities	Stocks
Net change	+3.2	+2.3	+0.9	+2.7
Close	1749.6	1390.2	238.8	1298.8
Previous day	1746.4	1387.9	237.9	1294.1
Week ago	1731.3	1412.7	239.0	1295.4
Month ago	1771.0	1447.1	243.4	1324.6
Year ago	1568.7	1436.3	231.5	1230.5
1989/90 high	1791.3	1918.1	250.3	1442.8
1989/90 low	1425.7	1271.7	196.3	1099.5
1988 high	1457.9	1421.2	198.8	1117.9
1988 low	1212.0	1034.7	175.3	939.5

Figure 3. The Indexes

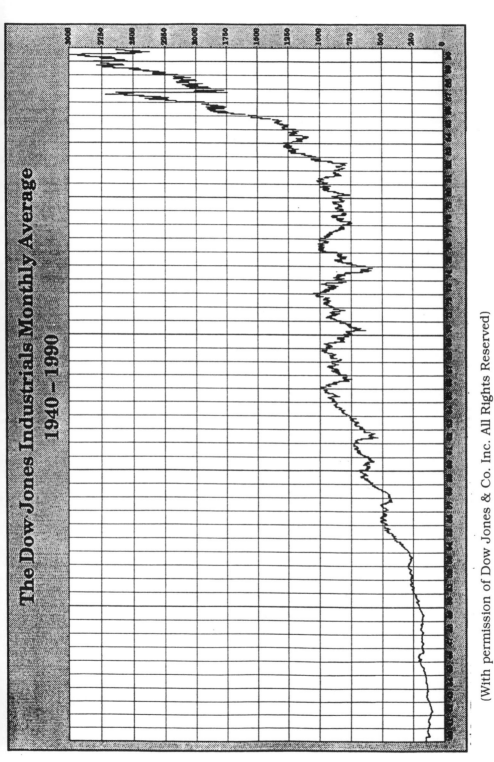

(With permission of Dow Jones & Co. Inc. All Rights Reserved)

Figure 4. The Dow Jones Index

Market Breadth Index is the only non-price index. Market Breadth compares the number of stocks that declined in price with the number of stocks that have advanced. There is a theory: it says that if the Dow Jones is up and if the Market Breadth is also up, then you can probably predict that the price will go up the following day.

The Standard and Poor Index is argued to be more accurate than the Dow Jones because of the five hundred stocks it represents rather than thirty.

There is one business daily in Canada, The Financial Post. The Globe and Mail is also renowned for its daily coverage of the markets. There is one Canadian business weekly, The Financial Times. All of these are published in Toronto.

In the United States, there is an important, well-known paper published by Dow Jones, The Wall Street Journal. It is very complete with regard to the New York and American Stock Exchanges. The New York Times Sunday Edition gives a complete rundown of the major U.S. exchanges. It is important for us because it can usually be picked up in any major centre and gives us the same information, available to everyone in the world, at the same time. I use it for closing prices of the previous

Friday. It is right up to date. Often, <u>Barron's</u> comes out at the same time; it is a very readable paper and is most helpful in bringing any investor up to date with the latest developments of the major U.S. markets.

Lesson 2
The Convertible Security

Stocks and Bonds

With common stocks you own equity in a company. You are part owner. You have a vote. When you are a bond owner, you are a creditor of that corporation. (Figure 5). They borrow your money and pay you interest in order to use it. When the maturity date comes, they are obliged to pay back that debt. Bonds are usually issued in values of $1,000.00 and regardless of what you paid (bonds often sell at a discount), the corporation owes you the face value of the bond, plus any interest you have earned on the maturity date. This principle is extremely important. The bond is a senior security. If the corporations should declare bankruptcy (which is relatively uncommon for a listed company), the bondholder must be paid in full before the common stockholder receives one cent. As a bondholder, you are in a much sounder position. Some brokers may try to persuade you to buy common stock, but as you will see, this might not be in your own best interest.

Canadian corporate bonds are sold 'over-the-counter'. Some are listed regularly in The Globe and Mail. The interest on bonds never changes, it is always based on $1,000.00 (which is par value). In fact, the interest is included in the name of the bond.

127

1. **HOLDER OF COMMON STOCK IS AN OWNER OF THE CORPORATION**

2. **HOLDER OF A BOND IS A CREDITOR OF THE CORPORATION**

Figure 5

The date given occurs when the corporation must pay the $1,000.00. For example, the name of the company might be "Rob M Blind 9-1/4 of 95", 9-1/4 is the interest rate; 95 means 1995, the maturity date. Always quote the interest rate and the maturity date as part of the name of the bond, as there is often more than one bond issued with the same corporate name. The interest rate is the same as the coupon rate. Bond prices are quoted as a percentage. Simply add a zero, for example, 85 becomes $850.00. The interest rate and the due date are important to quote to your broker when you place an order, so that there will be no misunderstanding.

Special bonds, such as the convertible bond, are the same as any other bond. That is, they are a senior security, they pay interest every six months, and they have a maturity date. However, there is one important difference. A convertible bond can be converted into common stock at any time up to the maturity (or expiry) date of the conversion privilege. Once you exchange it for common stock, the bond no longer exists. (It does not work the other way, i.e., you can not convert common stock into a convertible bond). Because it is a convertible, we enjoy the best of both worlds. A lot of small investors are not familiar with it. Remember, never buy a common stock without looking at the convertible bonds.

A convertible bond takes precedence over the common stock, both practically and psychologically. (Figure 6). It holds up better than common stock in a bad market. It has the luxury of being a bond, but is convertible into a predetermined number of stocks. It commands lower commission rates. Typically, you should pay no more commission than $5.00 to $15.00 per bond. But remember, every investment house has a minimum commission. Commissions vary from investment house to investment house. You should realize, as well, that some investment houses tend to discourage the small investor. Even though you might pay only $5.00 to purchase a convertible bond, had you purchased the underlying stock, you might have paid six or seven times that amount. It is important that you learn to make your own decisions; you must not depend upon a broker to make them for you. Remember, the broker would earn more commission on the purchase of common stock. But you'll have little trouble buying convertible bonds when you make your own decisions. Remember, never buy common stock without looking at the convertible bonds.

Margin

Margin is simply a credit agreement with your broker, and is relatively easy to obtain. There is in Canada a Canadian Securities Commission Regulation that states you must

ADVANTAGES OF THE CONVERTIBLE BOND

1. **SENIOR STATUS OF CONVERTIBLE BOND OVER THE COMMON STOCK**

2. **CONVERTIBLE PRIVILDGE TO EXCHANGE THE BOND INTO A PREDETERMINED NUMBER OF COMMON STOCK**

3. **LOWER COMMISSION RATES**

4. **LOWER MARGIN REQUIREMENTS**

5. **DOWNTREND RESISTANCE OF THE CONVERTIBLE BOND**

Figure 6

pay (put up) 50 percent of the market value of the common stock. With convertible bonds, you will only have to put up 20 to 25 percent of the market value of the bond. For example, for a bond priced at $1,000.00 you are normally required to put up only $200.00 to $250.00 of the value of the bond. It would not be wise to use much less than 20 to 25 percent margin because of the possibility of a margin call, i.e., a demand from the broker for money to support a possible investment loss, even though it may be temporary in nature. Remember that a convertible bond purchased at under $1,000.00 must return to $1,000.00 at the maturity date. As you will see, we always keep this point in mind when we are making our selection The same rules apply to American convertible bonds when you deal through Canadian investment houses. In the United States, investors have to put up 50 percent for bonds. American investors sometimes have accounts in Canada, and Canadian addresses, to benefit from the Canadian regulations.

There are many more American convertible bonds than Canadian, and we will look at them shortly.

Convertible Bonds and Underlying Stock

We are going to look at a graph that will give a picture of what happens with the convertible bond and help us to determine the best time to buy a convertible bond. Remember, we are not going to fall in love with any corporation. Don't be like the conservative investor who, lying on his death-bed, turns to his executor and pleads "whatever you do, don't sell my O. M. stocks, they have been with me for so long!" We are looking at timing. We will fall in love with situations.

On the right of the charts (Figures 7 and 8), the figures represent the price of the bond (and remember that it is represented as a percentage, so add a zero). Time moves from left to right. The heavy line at the top is the movement of the convertible bond. The fine line at the bottom is what the common stock would be worth at conversion.

Basic Terms:

Conversion Value is the value of the underlying stock if you convert. **Premium** is the difference between the market price of the convertible bond and the price of the underlying stock, or the conversion value. Use a percentage so you can compare one situation with another.

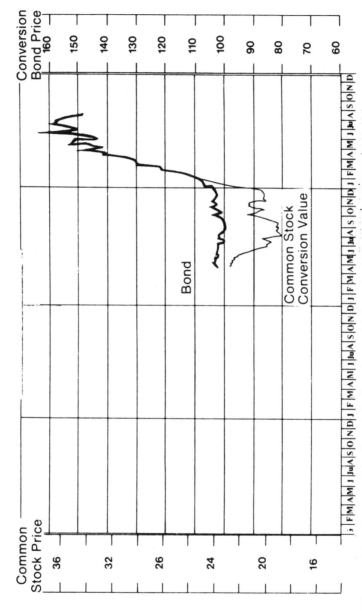

Figure 7. Convertible Bond Action in an Uptrend — Missouri Pacific 8%-'95

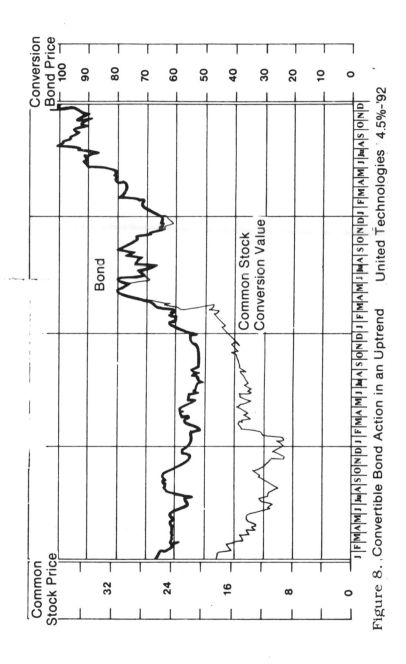

Figure 8. Convertible Bond Action in an Uptrend   United Technologies   4.5%-'92

How to Calculate the Premium as a Percentage

We buy a bond with a market price of: $900.00

This bond is convertible into stock
currently worth: $600.00

Difference: $300.00

To get a percentage to compare:

$$\frac{\text{(Difference)} \quad \$300.00}{\text{(Price of Stock)} \quad \$600.00} \times 100 = 50\%$$

How to Calculate Conversion Value

Multiply the number of shares by the market price of the stock.

What is the Ideal Time to Buy, Based on Our Criteria?

We want the smallest premium possible, preferable less than 15 percent. The ideal time to buy occurs when the premium is low. We do not try to predict. Even the economists cannot agree, but as cowboy philosopher Will Rogers noted, "they have as much right to guess as anyone". If you play the game of prophesy, certainly do not do it with real money.

Timing is critical. Assume, then, that we buy a convertible when the premium is low. If the stock goes up, the bond has to go up automatically in step with the common stock. Therefore, we have all the action on the upside in the same way as we do with the common stock. The traders, of course, know this.

On looking at our examples in Figures 7 and 8, we see that the convertible bond is tied to the common stock. (Top line is the convertible bond, bottom line is the conversion value). The convertible bond must go up with the gain in the common stock, because you can convert into common stock anytime you decide.

It is important to buy the bond when there is little premium. In a bear market (downtrend), stocks can fall but the bond will usually hold up (Figures 9 and 10). Remember, the bond is a senior security and the bondholder must be paid in full at maturity. As well, the bondholder collects interest. Even though MGIG fell to $700.00, the bondholder knows it has to go back to $1,000.00 when the maturity date is reached, as long as the company remains viable.

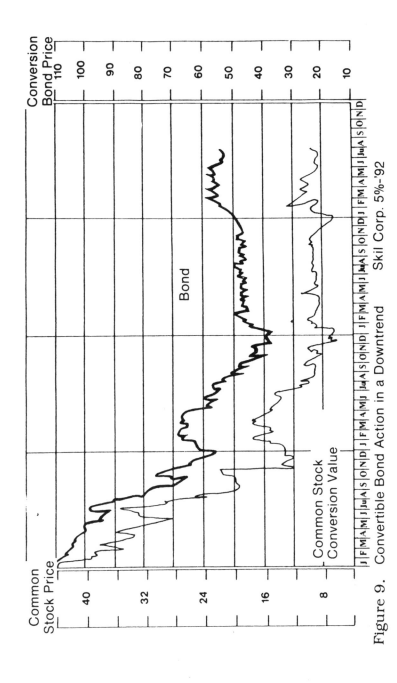

Figure 9. Convertible Bond Action in a Downtrend   Skil Corp. 5%-'92

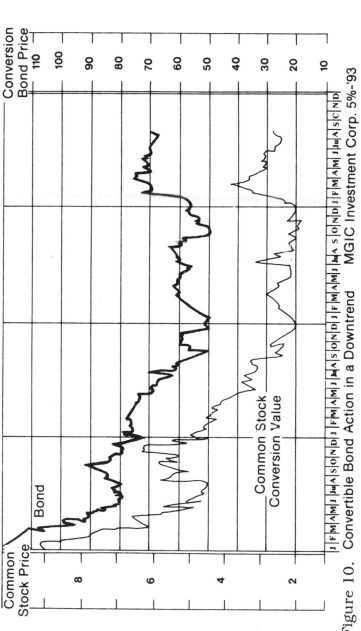

Figure 10. Convertible Bond Action in a Downtrend   MGIC Investment Corp. 5%-'93

Why Buy a Bond at Close to or Under $1,000.00?

Because the resistance on the downside starts at around par value. Under $1,000.00 the bond starts to resist the descent of the market. If you bought the bond at $1,600.00, the price of the bond would be likely to fall with the price of the stock.

Now we Have Two Rules:

1. Look for a low premium. In case the stock goes up, we want all the action.

2. Buy at close to $1,000.00 or under in case the bond price slumps. That will give us resistance on the downside.

Bonds can fall in price, but I want to emphasize the advantage of holding convertible bonds as opposed to common stock. Bonds resist the downtrend. Even though the price may be low, it must go back to $1,000.00 at the maturity date.

No one knows which way stock is going to move, so it is comforting to have the resistance of the convertible bond. In addition, the convertible bond can have all the action of the common stock on the upside, while it also pays interest.

Lesson 3
The Ice-Breaker Exercise

It is recommended that you do this exercise as described. The results of the sample class are discussed later based on the same figures. Set up your choice in the "Ice-Breaker Exercise" format. (Figure 11)

The Profit-Taker system will never be completely computerized -- there is always a certain amount of subjective human intelligence required. Not all of the criteria have an absolute weight. Common sense is necessary.

Not all the information that one needs is available in financial newspapers. Other sources are necessary. One excellent source is <u>Value Line Convertibles</u>, (220 East 42nd St., New York, N.Y., 10017, U.S.A. Telephone 1-800-833-0046) which is a weekly publication.

I want you to select four convertible <u>bonds</u> in the order that you would buy them based on the following criteria:

1.   **Premium** (Figure 13, Column 34, <u>Value Line</u>) under 20 percent. (You want to get all the action of the common on the rise. The lower the premium, the better).

141

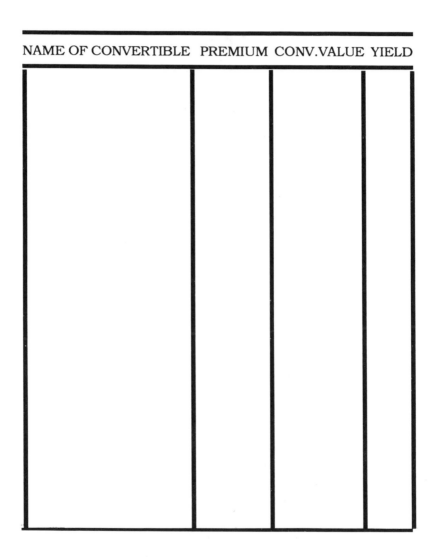

NAME OF CONVERTIBLE	PREMIUM	CONV.VALUE	YIELD

Figure 11. Format of Ice-Breaker Exercise

2.   **Conversion Value** (Figure 13, Column 33) $1,000.00 or under. If the bond goes down, you want resistance on the downside. The lower the conversion value, the better. Give this equal weight with the premium.

3.   **Current Yield of the Bond** (Figure 12, Column 7) The higher the yield, the better. With this strategy, we are not likely to hold the bond to maturity.

Remember to list the name of the bond (Figure 13, Column 24) with the coupon and maturity date, e.g., Advest Group Inc. 9% of 2008, on the form in Figure 11. Do this exercise, please, before reading further for the comments and results of the exercise.

Results of the Ice-Breaker Exercise

Now we are going to learn how to avoid a great many pitfalls. Remember, working with hot tips leads to disillusionment. We will start with a brief review of the basics.

Let's summarize the highlights. We have discussed the difference between holding a common stock and a bond. Stock means ownership. Stockholders are responsible to the

143

COMMON / CONVERTIBLE FACTS

BONDS & PFDS

SYMBOL	EXCH	PRICE	PERF RANK	REL VOLAT (%)	YIELD (%)	CURR YIELD (%)	YIELD to MAT (%)	PAYMENT DATES	CONVERSION RATIO	BREAK EVEN TIME (MOS)	HEDGE RANK	RATIO	ISSUE SIZE	CALL PRICE *	VALID UNTIL	IF COMMON IS ($)	FOR THIS # OF DAYS	INDUSTRY	CY PAGE REF	EXCH	SYMBOL
BMD	A	22.13	1	145	13.1	6.5	6.2	Jd15	48.485	20	C	360	60.00	NCB	6/30/91	FCP 106.200		MedSup	290	N	BMD.F
AM	N	2.75	-	160	NiL	12.1	6.8	PFD FMAN15	2.985	50	C	68	3.450	26.200	2/14/91			PrcIns	322	N	AMPr
ASTA	O	16.75	2	220	NiL			Mn15	64.516	16	C	495	50.00	107.650	5/31/91	23.25	20/30	Cmptrs		O	ADBPrA
ADB	N	12.75	2†	25	NiL	.9	7	PFD FMAN15	1.064	35	C+	42	4.159	NCB	10/30/90	FCP 21.166		Petrol		N	AMDPr
AMD	N	9.38	2†	155	NiL	8.0		PFD MJSD15	1.987	50	C+	81	3.450	52.100	3/14/91			Semicn	314	N	
ADV	N	5.38	3	120	3.0	11.2	11.7	Ms15	73.706	74	C-	345	26.49	104.800	3/15/91			Broker		N	ADV.F
ARWS	N	10.75	-	140	NiL	8.9	9.4	Jd15	63.682	29	C	415	40.00	103.875	6/14/90	FCP 104.725		AirTrn	213	N	
ALK	N	23.63	4	110	.8	7.9	8.1	dJ15	29.762	47	C	190	75.00	NCB	7/1/92			AirTrn	350	O	ALKA.F
ALK	N	23.63	4	110	.8	8.0	8.1	Jd15	35.398	23	C	210	28.81	104.650	6/14/90			AirTrn	350	N	
ABSB	O	11.00	-	145	2.0	9.3	12.2	J12	38.417	53	C+	148	25.00	104.000	6/11/90			Broker		O	*EURO*
AAL	N	26.50	3	105	3.8	10.6	10.5	Ao15	25.641	61	C	38	67.60	105.870	4/14/90			Ins Dv	340	O	
AG	N	0.56	-	210	NiL	NMF		PFD JAJO	1.724	NMF	B	133	1.913	100.000				Mityfm	186	O	AGPrc
ALN	N	11.88	3	130	NiL	9.9	14.4	PFD FMAN	0.909	47	C-	58	2.300	26.225	5/14/90	59.63	20/30	AutoPt		N	ALNPrA
ALNT	O	6.25	-	130	NiL	13.6	14.4	Mn15	25.157	62	C	159	39.20	105.800	5/14/90	FCP 105.800		Cmptrs		O	ALNTG
ALWS	O	8.88	3	160	NiL	7.3	7.3	Jd	83.770	41	C-	575	30.00	NCB	5/31/91			Ind Sv	368	O	ALWSG
AA	N	63.75	3	95	2.5	5.7	5.1	May27	16.129	26	C	114	150.0	NCB	5/26/92	FCP 103.000		Mining		O	*EURO*
AZA	A	42.13	2	140	NiL	5.1	4.7	May8	24.004	13	C	174	75.00	103.000	5/7/90	55.25	20/30	Drug		O	*EURO*
AMX	N	28.25	3	125	2.8	6.9		PFD MJSD	1.310	45	C	86	0.235	50.000				Mining	060	N	AMXPrB
ADU	N	1.50	5	130	NiL	NMF		PFD FMAN15	1.709	NMF	A	48	1.100	21.170	12/14/90			MchCns	292	N	ADUPrD
AWAL	O	9.88	-	135	NiL	10.3	10.0	Jj	95.200	19	C	630	48.00	108.050	12/31/91	15.75	20/30	AirTrn	207	O	AWALI
AWAL	O	9.88	-	135	NiL	9.5	10.0	fA	74.074	13	C	540	37.35	104.650	7/31/93			AirTrn	207	O	AWALG
AWAL	O	9.88	-	135	NiL	9.4	9.9	Ao	71.429	14	C	510	36.15	104.500	3/31/91			AirTrn	207	O	AWALH.O
ABIG	O	10.63	3	100	4.7	9.7	9.0	jD	73.260	71	C	183	35.00	110.000	12/1/91	25.51	30	Ins Dv		O	
ABIG	O	10.63	3	100	4.7	6.7	7.7	May27	50.955	NMF	C	105	70.00	101.000	5/26/93	73.75	20/30	Ins Dv		O	*EURO*
AWAL	N	64.63	3	90	4.2	6.7	5.9	June15	17.637	5	C+	135	400.0	105.425	6/14/90			Tobaco	172	O	*EURO*
AMB	N	64.63	3	90	4.2	4.7	3.9	S8	17.241	73	C	112	200.0	100.000	9/7/93	75.40	20/30	Tobaco	226	O	*EURO*
AXP	N	26.00	3	95	3.5	7.8	7.5	Jd15	22.900	NMF	C-	140	59.80	NCB	6/14/94	FCP 103.250		FiniSv	292	O	
AGC	O	36.75	-x	75	4.3	5.8	4.5	May30	24.691	NMF	C-	109	300.0	101.000	5/30/90	52.65	30	Ins Dv	284	O	*EURO*
ABS	N	4.63	-	130	17.3	22.0		PFD FMAN	0.930	NMF	C-	34	2.500	25.875	4/30/90			Bank	064	N	ABNYP
ADD	N	4.38	4	150	NiL	19.7	20.7	ao	46.512	28	C+	145	135.0	NCB	10/15/92	FCP 105.250		RetStr	292	N	ADS.F

AMGEN	O	62.00	1	175	NIL	31	6.5	5.5	June30	19.379	6	C+	139	50.00	105.600	6/29/92	67.08	20/30	Chem	282	O	"EURO"	31
AN	N	53.25	3	70	3.6	32	6.3	6.0	mS	19.048	58	C-	141	498.9	NCB	9/1/85	FCP	102.210	Petrol	034	N	ANC.F	32
AAC	N	3.00	4	200	NIL	33	16.9	17.7	Jj15	57.143	56	C-	500	23.23	100.000	1/15/02			Cmptrs	340	N	AAF.F	33
APC	N	32.75	3	125	.9	34	5.9	5.0	M9	31.573	32	C-	220	79.97	NCB	3/8/92	FCP	104.900	Petrol		O	"EURO"	34
APC	N	32.75	3	125	.9	35	5.5	5.3	Mn15	29.240	40	C-	220	100.0	NCB	5/14/92	FCP	105.000	Petrol		O		35
APC	N	32.75	3	125	.9	36	5.5	5.3	Ao	30.651	13	C	230	100.0	104.025	3/31/91			Petrol		N	ANV.F	36
ANDR	O	10.25	-	135	NIL	37	12.7	13.4	aO15	61.856	22	B	225	9.900	105.250	10/14/90			Electr		O		37
ANT	N	12.88	-	110	3.4	38	6.9	3.4	jd15	126.580	2	C-	1180	21.95	100.000	1/31/00			Rec	015	A	ANT.A	38
ALG	N	23.50	3	80	4.6	39	6.5	PFD	MJSD15	1.747	67	C-	121	2.600	52.100	3/14/91			NatGas		N	ALGPrA	39
AS	N	10.13	3	155	NIL	40	9.4	PFD	MJSD	1.270	54	C	49	1.698	40.000				Steel	172	N	ASPr	40
AS	N	10.13	3	155	NIL	41	10.0	PFD	JAJO	2.220	60	C	62	1.000	51.800	6/30/90			Steel	172	N	ASPrA	41
ARW	N	4.88	3	160	NIL	42	14.1	PFD	FMAN	1.524	39	C	75	2.800	26.360	4/30/90			Electr		N	ARWPr	42
ARW	N	4.88	3	160	NIL	43	12.9	14.2	fA	28.736	75	C	124	30.00	102.250	7/31/90			Electr		A	ARWD.A	43
ARV	N	16.75	5	105	4.1	44	8.6	PFD	MJSD31	1.754	86	C	71	1.800	NCB	9/29/92	FCP	52.625			N	ARVPr	44
ASH	N	36.75	4	75	2.7	45	7.2	7.3	jJ	19.478	64	C	118	200.0	NCB	6/30/92	FCP	104.725	Petrol		O		45
ATL	O	4.25	-	135	9.4	46	9.0	10.4	Jd15	56.980	0	C-	305	17.25	104.450	6/14/90			FinlSv		N	ATL.F	46
ATC	A	5.75	-	175	NIL	47	9.7	13.1	Ap29	61.302	43	C+	305	75.00	103.000	4/28/90	21.20	20/30	Cmptrs		O	"EURO"	47
AAME	O	1.88	-	135	NIL	48	11.9	16.0	Mn15	91.408	76	C	395	30.00	105.600	5/14/90	16.41	20/30	Ins Dv		O	AAMEG	48
ADIE	O	9.25	-	110	NIL	49	12.0	12.9	Mn	28.881	54	C+	105	30.00	104.900	4/30/90			AutoPt		O	ADIEG	49
AVT	N	30.00	1	115	2.0	50	8.9	9.1	jj	19.231	63	C	72	100.0	103.200	9/30/90			Electr	364	N	AVI.F	50
AVT	N	30.00	1	115	2.0	51	6.5	6.6	Ao15	23.256	67	C-	152	115.0	104.800	4/14/90			Electr	364	N	AVT.F	51
BBTF	O	20.00	3	65	4.0	52	7.5	6.9	Mjsd15	56.338	11	C	410	34.50	104.375	3/14/91			Bank		O	BBTFG	52
BRE	N	26.50	3	60	9.1	53	9.8	9.9	Jd	32.258	NMF	C	156	50.00	103.800	5/31/90			REIT		N	BRP.F	53
BSN	A	6.75	-	90	NIL	54	12.8	15.5	Ao15	64.103	27	C+	200	17.50	104.430	4/14/90			Rec	319	A	BSNA.A	54
BHI	N	27.75	1	120	1.7	55	6.0	PFD	FMAN15	1.960	20	C	148	2.000	52.450	5/14/90	38.25	20/30	OlfdSv	285	N	BHIPr	55
BHI	N	27.75	1	120	1.7	56	8.9	8.7	jD15	16.975	92	C-	58	99.99	102.590	12/14/90			OlfdSv		N	BHB.F	56
BLY	N	12.63	5	130	2.4	57	13.2	PFD	FMAN	2.000	18	C+	96	2.000	52.800	1/31/91			Htl/Gm	244	O		57
BLY	N	12.63	5	130	2.4	58	9.3	13.3	mS15	34.495	56	C	112	31.61	100.000	8/14/98			Htl/Gm	244	N	BLY.F	58
BLY	N	12.63	5	130	2.4	59	13.7	14.5	jD15	30.600	49	C+	88	100.0	104.640	12/14/90			Htl/Gm	052	N	BLZ.F	59
BBCM	O	11.75	-	175	5.1	60	8.4	8.8	Ao	38.278	NMF	C-	163	22.12	104.050	3/31/91			Bank		O	BBCMG	60
BFL	N	9.75	-	100	4.5	61	11.3	12.2	aO	45.126	79	C	49	15.82	103.600	9/30/90			S & L		N	BFL.F	61
BKB	N	14.38	5	95	8.6	62	9.9	10.3	Jd15	42.699	NMF	C	166	95.28	104.650	12/14/90			Bank	364	O		62
BAS	N	0.19	-	140	NIL	63	NMF	NMF	Jd	88.732	NMF	C+	1080	30.41	105.250	5/31/90			Mltyfm	028	N	BAA.F	63
BMG	N	14.25	3	140	.7	64	6.3	6.6	Jan 4	48.484	57	C	295	100.0	NCB	1/3/95	FCP	106.000	Mining		O	"EURO"	64
BAX	N	24.00	2	95	2.7	65	4.9	PFD	JAJO	2.976	4	C-	260	10.82	NCB	11/25/90	FCP	50.000	MedSup		N	BAXPrB	65

Figure 12. Sample of Value Line Convertible

VALUE LINE CONVERTIBLES

Footnote	Name of Convertible	Price	Perf Rank	Rel Vol (%)	Over(+)/Under(−) Valued (%)	#	+50%	+25%	−25%	−50%	Conversion Value	Premium (%)	Stock Market Risk (%)	Bond Market Risk	I.V. Grade	Investment Value	Premium (%)	Change/Pt Common	Change/Pt Interest Rates
	A. L. Labs 7.75s2014	119.00	1	110	+2	1	+35	+17	−17	−30	107.27	11	95+	45	F	65	83	3.57	2.38
1	AM International $2.00	16.50	3	60	+3	2	+5	+3	−3	−5	8.21	101	15+	45	G	16	3	0.66	1.16
2	AST Research 8.5s2013	119.50	2	170	+4	3	+35	+17	−18	−35	108.06	11	150+	120	F	62	83	4.78	2.39
	Adobe Resources $1.84	18.88	2	60	−2	4	+20	+8	−5	−9	13.57	39	35+	25	−	16	18	0.38	1.13
3*	Advanced Micro Devices $3 Dep	31.25	1	65	−4	5	+17	+8	−4	−8	18.63	68	40+	40	F	27	16	0.63	1.88
	Advest Group Inc 9s2008	80.25	3	60	+6	6	+8	+4	−8	−13	39.62	103	25+	35	G	67	20	3.21	4.01
	Air Wis Services 7.75s2010	87.00		95	+2	7	+25	+13	−13	−23	68.46	27	70+	15	G	58	50	4.35	2.61
4*	Alaska Air Group 6.875s2014	94.25	4	65	+2	8	+25	+12	−12	−22	70.31	34	50+	15	E	62	52	1.89	3.77
	Alaska Air Group 7.75s2010	97.00	4	70	−2	9	+30	+15	−11	−19	83.63	16	55+	15	E	70	39	1.94	3.88
5	Alex Brown 5.75s2001	62.00	−	*70	−5	10	+19	+9	−4	−8	42.26	47	40+	30	G	54	15	1.24	3.10
6*	Alexander & Alexander 11s2007	104.00	2	20	+3	11	+6	+3	−2	−3	67.95	53	10+	10	D	101	3	0.00	5.20
7	Allegheny Intl $11.25 C	1.00	0−	210	+3	12	+45	+21	−18	−23	0.97	3	145+	65	L	NMF	NMF	0.00	0.71
8	Allen Group $1.75 A	17.63	−	80	+7	13	+17	+8	−12	−20	10.79	63	40+	40	H	12	47	0.53	0.71
	Alliant Comp 7.25s2012	53.38	1	100	+7	14	+5	+3	−7	−11	15.72	239	20+	80	J	45	19	1.60	2.67
	Allwaste 7.25s2014	99.00	4	100	+5	15	+24	+12	−14	−25	74.35	33	80+	20	F	61	62	5.94	3.96
9*	Aluminum Co of Amer 6.25s02	110.50	3	70	+1	16	+40	+18	−15	−25	102.82	7	65+	5	C	72	53	1.11	2.21
	ALZA 5.5s2002	107.00	2	105	−1	17	+40	+19	−15	−25	101.12	6	100+	5	D	65	65	2.14	2.14
	Amax Inc $3.00	43.63	3	80	−1	18	+30	+15	−13	−24	37.01	18	70+	10	E	28	56	0.87	1.75
10	AMDURA $1.95 Dep	3.13	03	165	−9	19	+25	+10	+0	−2	2.56	22	40+	125	K	NMF	NMF	0.66	0.09
11	America West 11.5s2009	112.13	−	115	+0	20	+30	+15	−13	−24	94.01	19	75+	40	I	70	60	6.73	2.24
	America West Air 7.75s2010	81.25	−	120	+3	21	+35	+17	−16	−30	73.15	11	85+	35	I	48	69	5.69	1.63
	America West Air 7.5s2011	79.50	−	120	+1	22	+35	+17	−15	−25	70.54	13	85+	35	I	47	69	4.77	1.59
12	Amer Bankers Ins Grp 9.75s2004	105.88	2	35	−1	23	+15	+6	−3	−4	77.84	36	20+	15	E	101	5	1.06	5.29
13	Amer Bankers Ins Grp 5.75s2001	86.00	2	35	−8	24	+15	+6	+0	+0	54.14	59	15+	20	E	83	4	0.86	4.30
14*	American Brands 7.75s2002	115.25	2	65	−2	25	+30	+15	−13	−23	113.98	1	65+	0	C	81	42	1.15	1.15
15*	American Brands 5.375s2003	114.76	2	60	−4	26	+45	+22	−10	−16	111.42	3	55+	5	C	93	23	1.15	2.30
16*	Amer Exp(Alleghany)6.5s2014	89.00	3	50	+3	27	+20	+10	−11	−19	59.54	49	35+	15	D	63	41	1.78	4.45
17*	American General 6.875s2000	119.00	0−x	25	+5	28	+19	+8	−9	−14	90.74	31	25+	0	J	100	19	1.19	0.00
18	Amer Savings Bank $1.8125 A	8.25	3	120	+5	29	+8	+4	−6	−8	4.30	82	20+	100	J	NMF	NMF	0.33	0.33
19*	Ames Dept Strs 7.5s2014	38.00	31	130	+7	30	+6	+3	−8	−8	20.35	87	20+	110	J	NMF	NMF	1.52	1.14

#	Security
20●	AMGEN 8s2004
●	Amoco 7.375s2013
21●	Anacomp 13.875s2002
●	Anadarko (Burlington) 7s2004
●	Anadarko Petroleum 6.25s2014
●	Anadarko Petroleum 5.75s2012
	Andersen Group 10.5s2002
22●	Anthony Industries 11.25s2000
23●	Arkla $3.00 A
●	Armco $2.10
●	Armco $4.50
24	Arrow Electronics $1.9375 Dep
	Arrow Electronics 9s2003
25●	Arvin Industries $3.75
26●	Ashland Oil 6.75s2014
27	Atalanta/Sosnoff 7.125s2001
28●	Atari 5.25s2002
	Atlantic American 8s97
	Autodie 7s2011
29●	Avnet Inc 8s2013
●	Avnet Inc 6s2012
51●	BB&T Finl 8.75s2005
	BRE Properties 9.5s2008
	BSN Corp 7.75s201
30●	Baker Hughes $3.50
31●	Baker Hughes(Hughes) 9.5s2006
32●	Bally Mfg $4.00 D
●	Bally Manufacturing 6s98
●	Bally Manufacturing 10s2006
	Baltimore Bancorp 6.75s2011
33	BankFlorida Finl 9s2003
34●	Bank of Boston 7.75s2005
●	BASIX Corp 8.75s2005
35●	Battle Mountain Gold 6s2005
36●	Baxter (Travenol) $3.50 B

Figure 13.   Sample of Value Line Convertible

creditors of the corporation. Bondholders are creditors. The bond is a senior security. In the case of liquidation, the bondholders will be paid full par value ($1,000.00) before the stockholders are paid at all. In this situation, however, it should be realized that the bondholder may receive only a part payment.

With convertible bonds, you can always calculate what the stock is worth. In the United States, many bonds are traded on an exchange in a similar manner to stocks. Convertible bonds can be exchanged for a predetermined number of common stocks. This privilege exists up to the expiry date of the bond. It has many advantages for us. It has senior status over the common stock. The owners are protected on the downside because they are creditors of the corporation, yet they still have the privilege of exchanging the bond into a predetermined number of stocks.

The commission on convertible bonds is $5.00 to $15.00 per bond, however, remember to take into account minimum commissions. If you purchase the stock that the bond represents, you may pay six or seven times that amount.

The bond holder collects interest every six months.

We're not here to criticize the brokers, but we will later learn how to select the best one for you. There should be no problems implementing orders to buy convertibles, but <u>you</u> have to make the decision. <u>You</u> have to be in control of <u>your own account</u>.

With convertible bonds, you are normally only required to put 20 to 25 percent margin on the price of that bond, e.g., if the bond price is $1,000.00, the margin you put up is $200.00 to $250.00 to own that bond. With common stock, 50 percent margin is required. More margin is required for stock under $2.00.

Previously, we looked at the graphs showing the action of the convertible bond and its underlying common stock. The heavy line represented the movement of the convertible bond, the light line represented the movement of the underlying common stock.

We were agreed that we will proceed on the assumption that no one knows which way the market will move.

We learned two important terms: <u>conversion value</u>, which is the value of the underlying stock, i.e., what the stock is worth if converted, and <u>premium</u>, which is the difference between the convertible bond and underlying common stock expressed as a percentage (so we can compare). For example, market value $900.00, conversion price $600.00, difference $300.00, expressed as a percentage, is 50 percent.

If we buy with a low premium and the stock goes up, the bond has to go up with the stock because it is convertible into common stock. If it doesn't, you could exchange your convertible bond for common stock. The traders are familiar with this feature of the convertible. The bond goes up in direct proportion to the stock. If you buy at the right time (low premium) with right action, it is very exciting. If you bought a bond with a large premium, for example of 50 percent, you would have to wait until the stock caught up to the bond in order to have substantial effect on the convertible bond. And we know that stocks don't always go up. In fact, we wouldn't be working this hard if they always did!

Rear-view mirror investing is easy. Every investor has heard the old stock market cliche, "if only I had got into IBM or Polaroid then". But remember, nobody back in those days knew those stocks would take off like a rocket, and out of dozens -- if not hundreds -- of stocks being promoted in those days, only a fraction of them were so wildly profitable.

More good news -- the bond resists the

downtrend. Prices hold up in the bond market. Even though it might be trading low, the bond must return to face value come maturity date. Everyone knows that it must go back up to $1,000.00. Common stock never <u>has</u> to go back. The convertible bondholder has the assurance that the bond price has to go back up.

We must also be realistic. In a bad (bear) market, the convertible bond can lose money as well. And we are going to do something about that shortly. We are going to see how we can get a kind of "insurance policy" or better in a descending market.

One other criterion that should be considered here is this: the closer the maturity date, the greater the resistance on the downside. The financial health of the institution is also important.

There are always situations which approximate our criteria. We are now doing the pre-selection, and will then bring our selections right up to date with information directly from our broker, or from current financial papers.

Well over one thousand convertible bonds are listed in <u>Value Line</u>. Once you know what you are looking for, you can locate the "live ones" very quickly.

It is easy to work with both American and

Canadian bonds. Remember, both American and Canadian bonds may prove to be very lucrative for the Profit-Taker Hedge.

Now let's look at the results of the Ice Breaker Exercise. The convertibles which met the criteria on pages V2 and V3 of <u>Value Line</u> (Figures 12 and 13) were:

NAME OF CORPORATION (Column 24)	PREMIUM (Column 34)	CONV.VALUE (Column 33)	YIELD Column 7)
1. American West Air 7.75 of 2010	11	73.15	9.5
2. American West Air 7.5 of 2011	13	70.54	9.4
3. BRE Properties 9.5 of 2008	13	85.48	9.8
4. Alaska Air Group 7.75 of 2010	16	83.63	8.0

Premiums are all less than 20 percent, conversion values are under $100.00, and the yields are very close. After balancing off the premium and the conversion value against each other and taking into account only these three criteria, I think I would choose American West Air 7.75 of 2010, although they are all quite similar.

Sources

As I said earlier, making the right selection entails a fair amount of work, but you will find that it is worth it. After making the selections and seeing the results, you'll know how to repeat your success.

It is like when you first learned to drive a car. When I was introduced to the clutch, brake, gas pedal, and steering wheel, I was sure that it was impossible to co-ordinate everything. This is the same. Once you know the criteria, you will find it to be a very lucrative experience.

We will now explore where we can get the information necessary for the Profit-Taker strategy. <u>Standard and Poor</u> and <u>Moody's</u> are both good sources. For the purpose of this personal seminar, we will use <u>Value Line</u>. It provides the same information as <u>Standard and Poor</u> and <u>Moody's</u>, which are monthly. <u>Value Line</u> is a weekly. It is often unnecessary to subscribe to <u>Value Line</u>, as it is usually available in libraries. You will have no trouble using these sources, once you know what to look for.

Now, as an example, we will look at the first pages of <u>Value Line</u> (V2 and V3). Treat these two pages as one. (Figures 12 and 13). Remember, no publication is set up exactly for our benefit, so I will explain the columns that affect the Profit-Taker selections. I have circled the columns that I am asking you to examine closely.

Evaluation of Common, is the section on the left hand side of V2 (Figure 12) that gives explicit information about the underlying common stock.

Name of Corporation is Column 24 (Figure 13).

You will note right away that there are two kinds of convertibles: convertible bonds and convertible preferred shares. The same principles apply to both, and you can do the same things with both. But the convertible bond is the senior security to the convertible preferred. The bond has a maturity date on which it pays $1,000.00 (par value). The convertible preferred has no maturity date, and that can work against us. On the downside, the convertible preferred often holds up like a bond, but often not as well as a bond. If a preferred is exceptional, using our criteria, I might select it; but in the interest of time, we are going to concentrate on the convertible bonds.

We can recognize the convertible preferred because the $ (dollar) sign is used. Yield to Maturity in Column 8 (Figure 12) specifies "PFD" so you should want to be aware of this column.

VALUE LINE COLUMN HEADINGS

The columns most relevant to this strategy are as follows:

Evaluation of Common (Figure 12)

Column 1: <u>Symbol</u> represents the symbol on the broker's computer. It is not important for you to remember it because the broker knows it or can look it up.

Column 2: <u>Exchange</u> "O" refers to "Over the Counter" and simply means it is not listed on any exchange. You should know what exchange the common stock is listed on.

Column 3: <u>Price</u> per Share of Common Stock.

Column 6: <u>Yield</u> is the dividend yield reduced to a percentage.

Convertible Facts (Figures 12 and 13)

Column 10: (Figure 12)

<u>Conversion Ratio</u> is the number of shares for which each bond can be exchanged, that is, how many shares you would receive if you converted that bond into common stock. You cannot have a percentage of a share. The figures are rounded, e.g., 9.868 becomes 10.

Column 21:   (Figure 12)
<u>Exchange</u> is the exchange on which the convertible trades. It is usually the same as the common, but not necessarily.

Column 25:   (Figure 13)
<u>Price of Convertible</u>. Remember, bonds are quoted in percentages; preferred shares are quoted in dollars.

Column 33:   (Figure 13)
<u>Conversion Value.</u> This is what the underlying common stock is worth if converted. You can check this by multiplying the number of shares by the price of the stock.

Column 34:   (Figure 13)
<u>Premium</u> is calculated the same way as has already been explained. (Page 133).

Column 7:   (Figure 12)
<u>Current Yield</u> is related to the interest. It's based on the current price of the convertible. Current yield is the interest that you receive based on the price you pay for the bond multiplied by 100 percent. If you pay less than

156

$1,000.00, you will receive more interest than the coupon rate.

For example, if a bond pays $60.00 interest yearly, even though you paid $800.00 for the bond, you will still get $60.00.

So the current yield is:

$$\frac{\$60.00}{\$800.00} \times 100 = 7.5\%$$

This column reflects the rate of interest based on the price of the bond rather than the par value of $1,000.00. It changes directly with the market price of the bond. Yields go up when the market price of the bond goes down. If the bond price is over $1,000.00, then you are going to collect less interest percentage-wise.

Column 8: (Figure 12)
Yield to Maturity. This column reflects the gain you receive by holding the bond to maturity.

Lesson 4
The Short Sale

The Short Sale

The short sale is a fascinating concept, but sometimes it is difficult to grasp at first because you have to think in reverse. Selling short is the opposite of buying a stock. Selling short means selling a security that the seller does not own. When I do seminars in Alberta, I do not have trouble explaining the short sale because I use the example of the rancher who sells his crop before he buys the seeds, not knowing what the final market price will be. The rancher here is only selling a contract. For some reason, if you talk about selling a stock you do not own, people become suspicious and ask: "Are you sure this is legal, do you think this is ethical, selling something you do not own?" I assure them it is absolutely legal, and it is certainly ethical, although taken by itself, it is not necessarily financially advantageous. I do not recommend it as an investment on its own merit, and you will see the reasons as we go along.

Alone, short selling is no better than buying a common stock. In my opinion, it may be a little worse. However, it is an important concept to understand because we are going to make good use of the short sale. Publishers, for

159

instance, sell magazine subscriptions when they have not even planned the cover - thereby selling something they do not own. Yet we send our money in good faith, and so, in effect, this is a short sale.

Selling short is a very common transaction. Six to eight percent of the transactions on the New York Stock Exchange are short sales, so it is not anything particularly unusual. There is no problem with the transaction. However, when I try to explain the short sale, it always comes back to "how can you sell something you do not own?" We are going to find out, right now.

Let's take this example. Your brother-in-law has designed a new kind of supermarket and has worked out all the details. This supermarket is quite different from anything that has been done before. This supermarket is going to allow the shopper an opportunity to relax and have a cocktail or a drink as the merchandise moves along temptingly on a conveyor belt. Your brother-in-law has everything he needs except capital, which he decides to raise by selling common stock.

The stock for his company, The Rob M Blind Corporation, is currently selling at $30.00 a share. Many investors feel that is overpriced, and the last thing they want to do is buy at

$30.00 as they think it is going to go down in price. If you really believed the price was excessive, you might want to profit by speculating on the possibility that the price is going to go down. Naturally, you would not buy at $30.00, but what you could do is sell short at $30.00. Why? Because you think the price is going to fall. (Figure 14).

So you approach this in reverse. Hoping you can buy it back later at a lower price, you sell short at $30.00 and you happen to be right, for it falls to $20.00. You decide to take your profit. What you do here in order to liquidate the short sale is to "buy in" or "cover" by buying shares at $20.00. By doing this, you have made a profit of $10.00 a share.

SHORT SALE

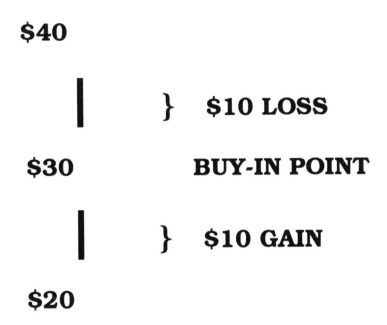

$40

} **$10 LOSS**

$30   **BUY-IN POINT**

} **$10 GAIN**

$20

Figure 14. Rob M Blind Example of the
Short Sale

We also know, however, that nobody can predict accurately which way any stock will move. What if it goes up to $40.00 instead of down to $20.00? You lose when it goes up, and you gain when it goes down. Just the opposite of the traditional way.

What if you decide to take your losses at $40.00? You buy in or cover. You bought at $30.00, therefore there is a $10.00 loss when the stock rose in price. When someone sells short, they are, in effect, being pessimistic about the future of the stock, believing the price is going to go down rather than up, and so they try to profit accordingly.

There are two kinds of investors basically, and there are books written for both types - the optimists and the pessimists. The optimists believe that stocks are going to go up - eventually. They might have gone down for the past ten years but the optimists believe they are going to go up in the future. Typically they will make comments like, "come the bull market, we are going to make a fortune".

Then we have the pessimists -- the short sellers -- who believe that the market is going to go down. Here are the people who believe that things are going to get so bad that you should dig a hole in the back yard, fill it with a year's supply of dried food, because the bottom is going

163

to fall out of the market. And when it does, they are going to make a fortune, but only if they are prepared. A lot of people subscribe to that philosophy. These basic kinds of thinkers don't change easily.

We are going to make good use of the short sale. For our purpose, all you have to know about the short sale is that you make money when the stock price goes down and lose when the stock price goes up. Now I want you to understand what happens when you place an order for a short sale.

By the way, I want to stress once again that your broker is not your financial partner. The investment house does not take any risks. When you buy on margin, they hold your stock. Don't get the impression that they are taking any risk, they're not. The stock, in effect, acts as collateral. If you profit, or make money, the profit is yours. Should you lose money, the loss is yours as well. They do not share in your loss or your profit.

You need a margin account to sell short. Even if you put up 100 percent of the money, you must sign a margin agreement in order to sell short. That's a regulation. It does not mean that you have to borrow money. There is a reason for this arrangement, which I will come to later. As when buying stock, when you sell short, you are responsible for putting up 50 percent of the market price of any stock priced over $2.00 in Canada. You can, of course, put up 100 percent, but you must put up at least 50 percent. You do not pay back the principal like you do a bank loan. You pay interest on it, usually a point or a point and a half over the prime bank rate.

Let me tell you something that is worth the price of this book many times over, and a great many investors do not appreciate what I am going to say right now. As already stated, if you sell short you must put up 50 percent of the price of the common stock. **If you execute a short sale of the underlying stock of a convertible security you hold, you are not required to put up any money whatsoever**.

Let me give you an example. Let's assume the market price of a convertible bond is $1,000,00 (the current market price). Let's say you want to use margin, so you put up $200.00 to $250.00 to buy the bond. If you wanted to sell the stock that the bond represents short -- we will see why you might want to do this as we move along -- you will not be required to put up any money whatsoever. And there is a good reason for this. We are going to see that by selling short, you are making the bond more secure. You are taking out the risk associated with that bond on the downside.

I would like you to have an appreciation of what happens when you give your broker the order to sell short. Here is the principle that is involved. (Figure 15). You are the short seller.

You want to sell short 10 shares of Rob M Blind. You would go to your broker, Broker A and say, "Sell short 10 shares of Rob M Blind". That's all you have to do.

What does he have to do? Remember you had to sign a margin agreement? This margin agreement permits the broker to lend your stock out for the purpose of selling short. There is a regulation that states that if you sell short the broker must have the respective stock in his physical possession. So, where does the broker get the stock?

Here's how it works. To get it he goes to his margin account inventory to see whether he has any of that specific stock. He checks his margin accounts and finds none. So where does he go? He goes to the common pool. He goes to Broker B and asks for Rob M Blind. Broker B looks through his inventory and finds that one of his accounts has some, which Broker A then borrows.

Broker B is delighted to lend the stock. Why? Because he receives cash -- the current price for that stock, and Broker B can use that

166

money for whatever he wants in the meantime.

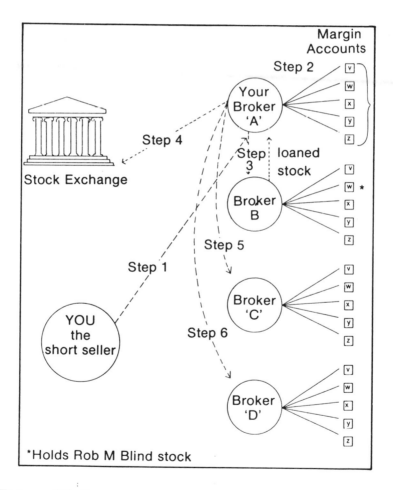

Figure 15 The Inner Operation of the Short Sale

Now Broker A has the stock. Broker A then goes to the exchange, making it clear to the exchange that this is a short sale and not the usual sale. The exchange sells that stock short in pretty much the same way as by a regular sale. When that is done, the broker calls you and tells you he has sold 10 shares of Rob M Blind. Everything is fine for a while.

I want to point out a situation that you can avoid. What happens if Broker B's customers decide they want to sell their stock. They phone their broker and place the order to sell. Broker B phones Broker A and says he wants the Rob M Blind stock back fast, because he has to sell. But remember, Broker A must also have that stock. So what does Broker A do now?

He doesn't call his client right away. What he does is to go back to the pool. He goes to Broker C who checks out his client inventory. There is no Rob M Blind stock there! Broker A then goes to Broker D. He does not have any in his inventory either. There appears to be a shortage of Rob M Blind stock. What happens?

Broker A calls his clients and says, "There's a shortage of Rob M Blind, you will have to cover or buy in within the next three trading days." This is technically called "the squeeze". It simply means there are not sufficient stocks around in order to borrow to maintain your short sale. We avoid this situation by asking our broker in advance if there will be any problems with the short sale. Any reputable broker has a restricted list, and he knows even before you sell short whether there are likely to be problems obtaining a stock.

A short sale is not like an option, not like a warrant, not like a put or a call. It does not have an expiry date. There is no reason for one. I have held short sales for years. There is no reason why you cannot hold a short sale for as long as you hold any common stock that you buy.

I conducted a seminar once at Elmhurst College in Chicago. There was a woman there who was very familiar with short sales and she offered this depictive analogy. Her story went: "It's very similar to a person who decides to mow his lawn, but he doesn't own a lawnmower. But he sees that his neighbour on the left has an impressive electric lawnmower. So he goes to that neighbour to borrow the lawnmower and proceeds to mow his lawn. The observant neighbour on the right notices what a great job the mower was doing and says: "What a wonderful lawnmower you have there. Would you consider selling it to me?"

The person mowing the lawn did a very

quick calculation. He had seen the lawnmower on sale at Sears for $190.00. So he said: "Sure, I'll sell it to you for $250.00." So it was sold for $250.00 to the neighbour on the right. Then the seller rushes down to Sears and buys this lawnmower on sale for $190.00 and returns the new mower to the neighbour on the left. He sold something he did not own and he made a profit of $60.00. If he had run down to Sears and they didn't have any lawnmowers, that would be a "squeeze" and there would be a problem.

There are a couple of things that I want to point out. First of all, I am going to look at the danger of the short sale. Remember, by itself, it is speculative. The odds are not in your favour with the short sale. If you sell short at $30.00 and you now know that it has to go down to make a profit, the maximum that you can gain by selling short is $30.00, which is a 100 percent profit. If the company goes bankrupt, you have only made $30.00 at most. And it is highly unlikely that the company will go bankrupt.

If you are wrong and the price goes up, how much can you lose? There is no limit. The odds aren't great, are they? And it is highly unlikely that the company will go bankrupt.

When you refer back to Figure 15, you will see that there is the usual buyer of the common stock, and there is the buyer of the stock which was sold short. If the corporation declares a dividend, the company doesn't care if you sold short because they have a listed holder of the stock (the usual buyer) and if you want to sell short, that's like a side bet. The corporation is not going to pay dividends twice. It is only going to pay to the legitimate owner. The dividend goes directly to the usual buyer.

The <u>short seller also pays the dividend</u> to the buyer involved in the respective short-sale. Therefore, short sellers do not like dividends because they have to pay them.

Another difficulty is one that we know about: the possibility of a "squeeze", when you could be asked to liquidate a situation before you want to. Avoid it by asking, in advance, if there are any restrictions in buying the short sale stock. I should emphasize that I have never been caught in a "squeeze", but you should know that it can happen.

A very important advantage that falls to the short seller is that you do not pay interest on the amount you borrow from the broker for the short sale. The broker cannot charge interest for the same stock twice, i.e., to the buyer of the initial sale and to the short seller on a margin account.

When you sell short it is a credit to your account. But you cannot use the money. It is an artificial entry. When you cover or buy in, that's a debit. When you sell short, your broker must wait until there is an "up-tick", which means that the stock goes up slightly in price, i.e., 1/8th of a point. You do not have to be concerned about this, but it is a rule that your broker will automatically follow, and of which you should be aware.

By the way, you pay the same commission to sell short as you do to buy common stock.

Lesson 5
The Typical Investor

We have covered the convertible bond and the short sale separately. I think it would be appropriate at this time to review the behaviour of the typical investor.

You might just know this fellow in this example. He has some market experience but he needs to learn that it's not the *bears* and the *bulls* that get you in the stock market. It's the *bum steers*. He will show us the approach most investors go about trying to profit in the stock market in a way that we are going to try to avoid. He succumbs to many of the pitfalls of investing, nonetheless, throughout he musters a sense of levity. It may be a very useful exercise at this point to go over the way the typical investor goes about making his decisions on a day-by-day basis.

First of all, this typical investor goes into the market without any specific plan. He's got a hot tip on the Rob M Blind stock, perhaps from his broker or his hairdresser. That doesn't matter. He's really excited about a seductive investment. But he doesn't have a structure. However, he's done his homework, or believes he has. He's studied the annual reports and he thinks he has some information that the whole world doesn't know yet. When they find out, "boy", is this stock ever going to go up.

He's "<u>researched</u>" his stock and he feels that it is a growth stock and that it should split. Normally, if a stock splits, that's good news. If a $50.00 stock splits into two $25.00 shares, there is a tendency for the price of that stock to rise. Psychologically, there is a greater attraction to a lower priced stock than to a higher priced stock. Most people like a split because it means that the price rises; what they don't like is when the stock falls apart.

Furthermore, the company is working on seven-day shifts and the reports say that this is likely to continue. Can you imagine what that will do for the stock? <u>So he buys.</u>

At this point in his investing career he is a "fundamentalist". He looks for solid information. He attempts to find information that perhaps is not well known to other investors and thus he has reason to believe, based on his research, that the stock will go up in price. However, we know that stock prices are psychologically, often emotionally, charged. But remember the stock market is bIzarre. Every time one investor sells, another one buys, and they both think they are shrewd.

So, let's follow through with our investor and see how he makes out. Here we see that the stock <u>falls in price</u>. The investor is already in the red. "So what?", he says. (This is very common, because investors tend to make excuses on a day by day basis). Here there are two market oracles "founded on a rock", they are, one; "never sell too soon", and the second; "it's never too soon to sell". The investor decides, "I'll sell on the next rally. I'll admit I'm wrong, but I don't want to lose, so the next time it rallies, I'll sell. After all, how can you lose your life savings on something called securities?"

What do you know? <u>It goes back up</u>. We know that the only thing you can count on is that stock prices fluctuate and this stock goes back up. (In this situation, the Profit-Taker would have gained on the fluctuation).

Do you know how hard it is to sell stock when the price is going up? Human nature being what it is, it is very difficult selling when everything's positive.

Now our investor says, "I'll wait until I break even. Then I'll take all my money out and sell".

<u>Woefully the price drops again</u>. He's in the "red" again. So he comes up with a new strategy. Perhaps you've heard this one: "What I'll do as the stock price declines is 'average down'. That is, I'll buy more of it, so I don't have to wait for it to go up so far to make a

175

profit". This is based on a theory that if you continue buying more as the stock goes down, it doesn't have to rise so far to make a profit. (But we know that with common stocks, unlike convertible bonds, the stock doesn't ever have to go back up again. Alas, it could be argued here that to make a small fortune in stocks, invest a large fortune).

<u>The stock continues to go down</u>. "I can't sell now, I've had too much of a loss". He has heard the prudent dictum, "invest for the short term, the long term is unpredictable", but he also knows the words of wisdom, "invest for the long term, the short term is unpredictable".

Can you understand the logic of this? I've heard it many times. I've even heard brokers say, "Don't worry, it's only a paper loss". Go down to the broker's office and try to take out your money. You'll find out whether it's a real loss or not. Of course this is a real loss, but for some reason, this guy refuses to admit it to himself.

So he hangs on.

<u>Sadly it continues to fall</u>. He banters with his broker, "How much further can it really go? I may have to switch brokers - from _stock_ to _pawn_." He remembers the market epigram, "never risk what you can't afford to lose", but

then again there is the stock saying, "a big risk is the key to a big gain". We know, don't we? We know where the bottom line is. All of a sudden he's not talking about his stock any more at work.

He can only muster an "OH" and he was overheard to say, "if this isn't a depression, then it's the worst boom in history," as <u>it dishearteningly continues to fall</u>. Now he doesn't know whether to "be patient and never panic" or "to be nervous and keep a close watch". I am sure you must have known people who bought a stock - it might have been a growth stock or a computer stock, and all you hear about is how much money they made, and then suddenly for some reason, everything becomes quiet.

If you don't hear about it at all, it usually means that the stock has turned around and is falling.

This chap isn't talking about it anymore. Now he rarely mentions it, even to his wife.

<u>Devastatingly it continues to fall</u>. So he rationalizes, "how much further can it go?" Perhaps I should have "been flexible and changed courses" or should I now "be steadfast, and keep a steady course? What if I had bought it at this point, look at how much money I would have

made. But nevertheless, I'll hold it because it can't fall much further".

But we know differently, don't we?

Finally, he's losing a great deal of sleep. The pressure is on and it's simply not worth it to hold on to this stock any longer. He phones his broker and says, "Get me out of this. Sell my stock!"

In a bullish market when prices are going up, greed sets in, but in a bear market such as this, where the stock price is going down, fear sets in. Possibly it could go to zero, and often stock is sold at the worst possible time. Why? Because, unlike the Profit-Taker situation, there is no structure. Our investor has no plan. He did not know when he was going to buy or sell when he set up this common stock situation. So here he sells.

However, he has the habit. When he goes home at night, what do you think is the first thing he does? He picks up the paper to ponder the current price of his stock. He can't resist looking at it after he sold it. He wants to see whether or not he sold it at the "right" time.

What do you know? It moves back up again. He says, "I don't care. I wouldn't touch that dog again". Nevertheless, he continues to watch it.

The stock goes back down again. He says, "you see, I was right. It is a dog". But he still ogles it.

Then suddenly it goes up and comes down again. And he notices something. He observes "levels of resistance" where the stock doesn't seem to want to go any further - both on the upside and downside.

"I think I've got it. I think I've got the formula!"

He becomes an expert in the patterns that have formed from the refuge of the stock. This is called being a technician. Now he studies graphs and he has all kinds of words for his patterns, e.g., "heads and shoulders" and "lines of resistance". He believes that if you can really appreciate these graphs, you can predict which way the stock is going to move. Basically, he is saying that the stock has a memory, and he concludes that he has the answer. He is convinced that as long as the stock is trading in the right range, that he will make a fortune. That is, when it reaches the bottom line of resistance, he'll sell it.

So he decides to try again and to buy it here.

Let's see what happens.

It worked the first time as <u>the stock</u> <u>fluctuated</u>. Like Pavlov's dogs, every once in a while the investor is "conditioned" with a little reward. He's remunerated here because it happened to go up and now he presumes that he has the answer. "This is going to make a lot of money. I'm going to buy at the low price range and sell at the high price range."

There's one problem with this. Let's take a coin. The financial centre of Princeton University had graphs drawn up on the basis of the flipping of a coin. And it's amazing how much the graphs of the coin toss resemble those of the stocks.

Flip the coin. If it turns up heads nine times in a row, what are the chances of it coming up heads for the tenth time? That's right, fifty percent. The coin doesn't remember what the pattern was before. Stocks are no different. They don't recall where they've been. To try to say that a stock will remember where it's been and to profit from that is a bit impalpable, to say the least.

Many investors, at some time in their career, fall into this trap. And there are many newsletters that promote this technical approach to buying and selling stock.

Anyway, our typical investor decides he has the answer. <u>The stock goes back down</u>. "Yippee, I'll buy it again! I've got it this time."

<u>It starts to move up out of the "stock range"</u>. While it moves up he has a great idea. He's no dummy! He knows what a short sale is. So he comes to the conclusion that he could sell short at the top of the price range and double his profit by profiting as well on the downside. So that's what he elects to do. He sells short.

<u>What actually happens here is that the stock continues to rise.</u> "What rotten earnings, it's breaking out" he mumbles, i.e., it doesn't do what it is supposed to do. Should he subscribe to the sage epigram, "cut your losses, and take your profit as soon as you can", or the formula, "let your profits run". "If it goes up, I'll sell short more stock as it continues to climb, and then it won't have to fall so far to make a profit...", he speculates.

Sounds familiar? As a matter of fact, he's even got a name for it, he calls it "profit inversion". "If it drops", he says, "and I break even, I'll cover." But he still has no structure, no plan.

<u>As it advances</u>, he says, "how much higher

can it go?" We know, don't we? To any price.

 It continues to rise. All of a sudden, he's not talking at all about it any more. This is not psychologically healthy.

 The advance persists. Again, he can only muster an "OH". Notice the reverse resemblance of the trading pattern on the upside compared with the previous downside action.

 Then he has the audacity, as the price unabatedly climbs, to either blame *Lady Luck* and say, "why am I so unlucky?", or his stockbroker and say, "I'll call him my '*broker*' because when I listen to him, that's what I am."

 Finally in desperation, he calls his broker and says, "I've had enough! I used to be *bullish*, then I was *bearish*, now I'm *brokish*. Take me out of this. I want to buy-in".

 This is a classical example of how most investors go about speculating in stocks and bonds. Little wonder that some people make all the money when they have a structure and a plan, such as the Profit-Taker Plan. Others who make their decisions on a day-by-day basis or make their decisions based on greed or fear, eventually lose. -- And I don't think that this is an extraordinary situation -- do you?

Lesson 6
The Full Hedge

The full hedge: the marriage of the convertible bond with the short sale.

I would like to try an experiment that I think will prove to be very exciting. We all know what a convertible security is, and we all know what a short sale is. Let's try something. I told you that if you sold the security short that the convertible preferred or bond represents, you are not required to put in any investment money whatsoever, nor are you required to pay any interest. Let's try an example.

Commit this to memory: I will use this situation for the rest of the text and it will assist you to make money regardless of whether the price goes up or down. This is a straight-forward situation in the Rob M Blind Corporation. (Figures 16 and 17).

There is no premium on the convertible bond. Each bond is exchangeable into 30 shares of Rob M Blind stock. The Rob M Blind common stock is currently available at $30.00 per share. It is only a coincidence that the $30.00 and the 30 shares are the same number. It will help you to remember. Multiply the 30 shares by $30.00 per share and get $900.00, or what the bond is worth.

183

THE SITUATION IS:

NO PREMIUM ON THE CONVERTIBLE BOND

EACH BOND IS EXCHANGEABLE INTO 30 SHARES OF ROB M BLIND STOCK

ROB M BLIND CONVERTIBLE BOND IS CURRENTLY SELLING AT $900.00

ROB M BLIND COMMON STOCK IS PRESENTLY AVAILABLE AT $30.00 PER SHARE

Figure 16

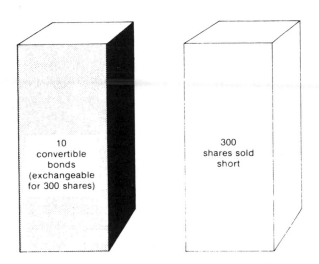

Figure 17. The Full Hedge

Let's go out and buy 10 bonds. This will represent a total investment of $9,000.00. Our broker phones us and tells us our order has been executed. Now, let's sell short all the stock that the bond represents. Each bond represents 30 shares. Ten bonds therefore represent 300 shares. Let's sell short all those shares. A simple transaction. Now we are not, of course, selling short the bond, but the 300 shares of Rob M Blind common stock. We have not used any money whatsoever for the purchase of the short sale. The only cost is the commission.

Let's see what would happen, and why we would even want to do this. First of all, this convertible bond is no different from any other convertible bond. It is typical. In a good market, with no premium, it has to advance directly with the movement of the common stock because it is convertible into that common stock. If the stock goes down, the convertible resists the downtrend because it is a senior security that bears interest every six months and pays $1,000.00 on the maturity date. So, if the convertible goes down, it defies the downtrend.

Let's say, first of all, that the stock goes up, i.e., there is an uptrend. It goes to $60.00. Let's understand where we would be if the common stock went from $30.00 to $60.00. (Figures 18 and 19)

186

FULL HEDGE-UPTREND

LOSS ON YOUR 300 SHARES SOLD SHORT
(300 SHARES SOLD SHORT X $30 ADVANCE)

$$= - \$9,000$$

GAIN ON EACH CONVERTIBLE BOND OF $900.00
(300 SHARES X $30.00 ADVANCE)

$$= + \$9,000$$

CONSEQUENTLY, NO LOSS ON THE UPSIDE

Figure 18

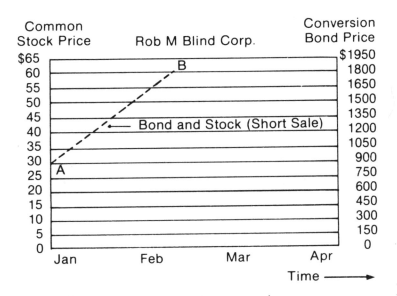

Figure 19. Uptrend Price Action of The Full Hedge

First of all, we have a loss on part of our transaction. Do we have a loss on our convertible bond, or on our short sale? The answer: on the short sale. How many shares did we sell short? The answer: 300 shares. Each advanced $30.00, from $30.00 to $60.00. So we have a loss of $9,000.00 on our short sale (300 shares times $30.00). However, our bonds also represent 300 shares. So with the $30.00 gain per share, we have a total gain of $9,000.00.

Let's subtract our gains from our losses. We have no loss on the upside, but also no gain. This is called a full hedge. We did not take any risk on the stock because one side balanced off the other side.

We didn't gain anything, but we didn't lose anything. Why should we want a full hedge? What would have happened had the stock fallen?

Now go back to the same situation. We bought 10 bonds for $900.00 each. Each bond represents 30 shares. We sold short all 300 stocks at $30.00. Let's say this time they dropped from $30.00 to $15.00. What would happen? (Figures 20 and 21)

Would we have gained on our bond or our short sale? The stock declined in price $15.00 each, so we gained on our short sale. Our bond

189

FULL HEDGE-DOWNTREND

GAIN ON YOUR SHARES SOLD SHORT
(300 SHARES SOLD SHORT X $15 DECLINE)

= + $4,500

LOSS ON EACH CONVERTIBLE BOND OF
$150 ($900 - $750) OR A TOTAL LOSS OF
(10 BONDS X $150)

= $1,500

OVERALL A **GAIN OF**

= + $3,000

Figure 20

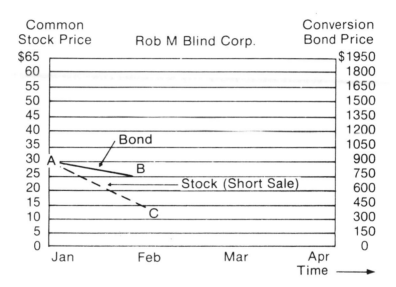

Figure 21. Downtrend Price Action of the Full Hedge

was a very representative convertible bond. It held up and formed a premium on the downside, however it did fall. From $900.00 it fell drastically to $750.00. So where did we lose money?

We had a gain of $4,500.00 on the short sale, but we had a bond that fell from $900.00 to $750.00. We lost $150.00 per bond, and remember we had 10 bonds, so we had a total loss of $1,500.00. Subtracting our loss from our profits, we had a gain on the downside of $3,000.00. This is not slight of hand!

What we have done is render the premium that inevitably forms on the downside into a profit for us, without taking any risk. This is the principle that allows the exchange to let us set up a short sale without putting up any investment money, because it made our bonds even more secure. I cannot imagine a more secure investment than the full hedge.

So, we have made a $3,000.00 profit, but what is wrong? It did not suit my temperament. I believe nobody knows whether a stock will go up or down. If the stock goes up in a full hedge, it's boring -- there is no gain and no loss. On the positive side it was risk-free, and I was making some money with the interest on the bonds. You can profit from the current yield on the upside, if the yield is higher than what you are paying for margin privileges.

On the downside, I found that it also took a great deal of time for the premium to be substantial enough to liquidate the situation. I am not discouraging anyone from using the full hedge as it is ultraconservative. Let's go on now and try a different approach in the next lesson.

Further actual examples of the full hedge are in the Appendices, page 254.

Lesson 7
The Half Hedge

The half hedge: grooming the convertible for the uptrend.

Let's start from the beginning. Everything is the same. The bond is $900.00, the stock is $30.00. The bond is exchangeable for 30 stocks and there is no premium. This time we'll do something different with our investment. Instead of selling short all 300 of our shares, sell short 150 of them. We call this a half hedge. We have 300 shares represented by the 10 bonds and 150 shares sold short. (Figures 22 and 23). What happens then when the stock goes up, and what happens when it goes down?

When it goes up.

Let's say, first of all, that the stock goes up from $30.00 to $60.00. The convertible bond has to go up because we can convert it into common stock anytime we like. Now what will happen? (Figures 24 and 25).

First of all, where is our loss? Do we have any losses? Yes, on the short sale. We have 150 shares sold short and they advanced to $60.00, so we lost $30.00 times 150, or $4,500.00 on the upside.

IN SUMMARY, HERE IS HOW IT LOOKS:
10 CONVERTIBLE BONDS AT $900 EACH
(EXCHANGEABLE FOR 300 SHARES)
                              = + $9,000

150 SHARES SOLD SHORT AT $30 EACH
(ONE-HALF THE FULL NUMBER OF
SHARES)
                              = - $4,500

Figure 22

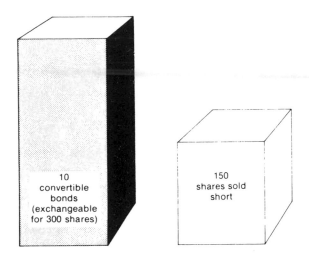

Figure 23. The Start of the Half Hedge

HALF HEDGE-UPTREND

**LOSS ON YOUR SHORT SALE
(150 SHARES SOLD SHORT
X $30 ADVANCE)**

= - $4,500

**GAIN ON YOUR CONVERTIBLE
BOND OF $900, SO, 10 BONDS
X $900 PROFIT
(300 SHARES X $30 ADVANCE)**

= + $9,000

SO, OVERALL PROFIT

= + $4,500

Figure 24

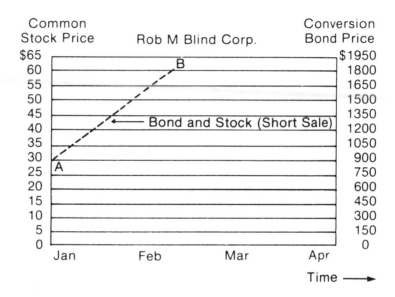

Figure 25. Uptrend Price Action of the Half Hedge

Where do we gain? On the bonds, because they had to go up as well, because they are tied to the common stock. We had a gain of $9,000.00 on the convertible bonds because the price went up, so a $30.00 advance for each stock times 300, is $9,000.00. Subtracting our losses from our profit, we have an overall profit of $4,500.00 on the upside.

Why? For incontrovertible reasons. There were 150 shares represented by the convertible bond that were not covered by the short sale and consequently those shares made money for us on the upside.

When it falls.

Let's go back to the same situation. Say this time that the stock fell from $30.00 to $15.00. Where would we have a gain on the downside? With our short sale or with our bond? (Figures 26 and 27). With the short sale. If we had 150 shares and they fell $15.00 each, we would have a $2,250.00 gain on the short sale. And our bonds fell as well! They resisted, but they still fell from $900.00 to $750.00, or $150.00 each. Even though we knew that they had to return to $1,000.00, they fell temporarily.

So we lost $150.00 on each of our 10 bonds, so the 10 bonds times $150.00, or a total loss of $1,500.00 on our bonds. Subtracting our losses from our profits, we have a profit of $750.00 on the downside.

HALF HEDGE-DOWNTREND

GAIN ON YOUR 150 SHARES SOLD
SHORT (150 SHARES SOLD SHORT
X $15 DECLINE)

                                    = + $2,250

LOSS ON YOUR CONVERTIBLE
BOND IS $150 EACH ($900 - $750)
SO, 10 BONDS X $150 LOSS

                                    = - $1,500

SO,OVERALL PROFIT

                                    = + $ 750

Figure 26

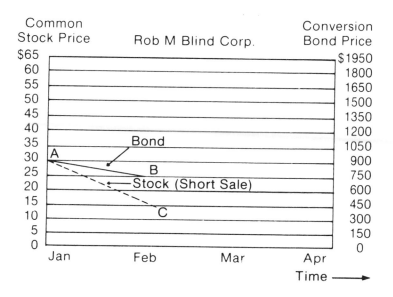

Figure 27. Downtrend Price Action of the Half Hedge

Why do we have that profit? Because we have two things working for us. We have the short sale and we have the premium which invariably forms on the downside on the convertible bond.

With this strategy, you no longer have to be afraid that the stock is going against you. In fact, most people who buy common stock often avoid active stock in case it reacts against them. They reason that by buying conservative stocks, at least they will lose money more slowly over a longer period of time. What's so exciting about that? You, on the other hand, will welcome action because you will feel confident that as long as there is action, this will create profits, regardless of the direction of the stock.

Lesson 8
Criteria to Select the Best Profit-Taker Candidates

So, look now at the Checklist. (Figure 28). Let's go over it. So far we have looked at three very important criteria. The Checklist in Figure 28 contains the entire list. We will learn how to set up a Profit-Taker Strategy. The Checklist has two columns on the right-hand side and a list of eight criteria on the left-hand side. The column labelled "Actual Rating" on the right will contain your own rating of your selection, and the second column from the right represents the "Suggested 100 percent Idea".

I am always looking for a 100 percent situation, but have never found it. If you found one which reached 100 percent, your next question would be, "what's wrong with this?" And that would be a fair question. We are looking for the most exciting current situation and we are going to rate it against the ideal, that is 100 percent.

It is generally recommended that you use the sequence of the criteria here as the process of elimination, in order to determine the most profitable situations.

Name of Security _____   Symbol_____

Rate and Maturity_____   Interest Date_____

Bond Purchased at_____   No. of shares (Short sale) _____

Date of Purchase _____   Price of stock share_____

No. of shares _____

	Suggested 100% Ideal	Actual Rating
1 __ The premium of the convertible under 15%.	10%	
2 __ Is the market price of the conversion value under $1,000 (par value)?	10%	
3 __ Of the situations being considered, how does the volatility of this common stock compare with the other candidates?	50%	
4 __ Consider the yield (%) paid *to you* by the bonds against the common stock dividends (%) paid *by you* on the short sales.	10%	
5 __ Does the company pay dividends on the stock?	5%	
6 __ A record of convertible premiums.	5%	
7 __ Does the company have assets in excess of the face value of the bonds?	5%	
8 __ Is the company in an industry in which there is a possibility of growth?	5%	

Figure 28. Abrams Automatic Profit-Taker Checklist
for Convertible Bonds

CRITERION 1:

The premium of the convertible is under 15 percent, which I give an evaluation value of 10 percent.

CRITERION 2:

Is the conversion price of the convertible under $1,000.00? This is a 10 percent value. The resistance usually starts in this area.

CRITERION 3:

I will discuss this shortly.

CRITERION 4:

Consider the yield. Compare the yield of the convertible against that of the stock. Who pays the common stock dividends on the short sale? You do, as the short seller. You do not want dividends here. Fortunately, most of the appropriate convertibles have underlying stock which pays little or no dividends. But always take a look at the dividends. Remember, you pay the dividends, but collect the interest on the convertibles.

CRITERION 5:

Does the company pay dividends on the stock? If they don't happen to pay dividends, give yourself full marks. That means you do not have to pay them on the short sale.

CRITERION 6:

A record of convertible premiums. When the stock went down, did the convertible hold up in the past? I know from a lot of experience (I can't think of one exception) that the bond fails to resist the downtrend in a bad market. But when you are first starting, I think it is comforting to know that the bond has a history of resisting on the downside. So I put this criterion in deliberately, so that you will check it out. You can get that information from your broker. Simply ask him if there has been any problem on the downside. Or, if you have historical graphs available, they should show the declining resistance of the convertibles.

Another practical way of doing this is to look up the low of the common stock for the past 52 weeks, say in Barron's, then calculate your conversion value. You know now how to do that, i.e., you multiply the number of shares by the market price of the low. Now take the low of the convertible bond for the 52 week period. It is usually available to you from the same periodical. Subtract this 52 week low figure of the convertible minus the low of the common stock value (expressed as a conversion value) and that gives you the premium in dollars. Then you calculate the premium as a percentage, the same way you calculated the premium previously.

For example:

52 week low of convertible bond	$700.00
52 week low of common stock	$ 20.00
Conversion value $20.00 times 30 shares	$600.00
Premium (The Difference)	$100.00

(i.e., the difference in dollars is the same as the premium in dollars).

Converted to a percentage, which will be:

$$\frac{\$100.00}{\$600.00} \times 100 = 16.6\%$$

This simple calculation gives you the minimum premium when the stock was at its low for the past 52 weeks.

CRITERION 7:

Does the company have assets in excess of the face value of the bonds? This is basic, fundamental information, and the best source is the Standard and Poor Stock Guide, which most brokers have on their desks. It is in most libraries. I only give it 5 percent and I ask you to look at this as a "worst scenario" situation. For example, if a disaster occurs and the company goes bankrupt, you should be confident that there are sufficient assets to cover the long term debts such as the convertible bonds. Most often they do. However, you should be aware if the company is in a precarious position.

CRITERION 8:

Is the company in an industry where there is a possibility of growth? Lastly, I have been good to you. I know that you have an itch to predict which way the stock is going to move. Here I give you 5 percent to go crazy. If the company is in an industry where there is a possibility of growth, for instance, you think that because the company manufactures horseshoes, and maybe horses are coming back, consequently the stock is going to skyrocket. But limit this to 5 percent of your total decision, because nobody knows for sure.

Remember, with this strategy, you make money on the fluctuations. Ideally you want it to reach your goal on the upside.

The most important criteria are the first two that we have already looked at: the premium under 15 percent and the conversion value under $1,000.00. Certainly, you should look at the yield and the dividend. As far as the record of convertible premiums and assets are concerned, these are nice to know and you should at least have checked them out before making your final decision. The parts I want you to be most familiar with are the first five criteria. I deliberately left one out until the end because it is so important and I want to concentrate on it alone, that is Criterion 3.

CRITERION 3:

Of the situations being considered, how does the volatility of a common stock compare with the other candidates? Why have my recommendations done so well? It is not because I have any special ability to predict which way a stock will move. I'm not surprised at the results, because I went out and looked for convertibles that had a very active underlying stock.

By the way, there is a column in <u>Value line</u> for volatility. That is not our volatility. There are other factors involved which do not relate directly to the price action of the underlying stocks. All we want to calculate is pure price action, not prophesies and other factors.

Let's focus now on volatility. Notice that I gave it a whopping 50 percent. (Figure 28). I did that deliberately in order to emphasize that this is the most important criterion. Although you should first satisfy the premium standards and the conversion value, there is no criterion as important as volatility. Volatility is simply this: the price action of the underlying stock.

How do we calculate it? The periodicals we will use will be based on 52 weeks. (There is nothing magical about 52 weeks, but that information is easy to obtain). For example, over a period of 52 weeks, the high is $60.00, the low is $30.00. Now we want to take a percentage so we can compare. We want the highest volatility that we can find. By the way, we can't buy the stock now for $60.00, we can't buy it for $30.00, because the market price is $40.00. <u>So our calculation must be realistic as to what we can buy at</u>. If we could buy it at $30.00, it would be much easier percentage-wise to double our investment than it is if we buy it at $60.00. If the price is close to the low, it is more likely to be volatile.

So we take the difference between the high ($60.00) and the low ($30.00), divided by the market price ($40.00), multiply it by 100 and get 75 percent volatility. That allows us to compare the volatility of one stock with another to select the one from which we can expect the greatest movement.

Sooner or later someone always asks, "what is good volatility"? It's a comparison and we're looking for the highest volatility. When do I get excited about volatility? My experience has shown that it is very much like the results of the exams you used to write in school. You know if the mark is over 60%, that's not bad. If it's under 50%, don't write home about it. If it's well over 70%, then that's really good news. The same is true with volatility, and you should have a winner as far as price action is concerned.

Sometimes a concern is expressed that volatility only spans 52 weeks. Maybe the company struck oil 52 weeks ago and had a high there, but nothing has happened since. That would be a fair comment, wouldn't it? What I do is start with the 52 week volatility, but before I make my final decision, I do my volatility for a period of twelve years, for a period of two years, for a period of the last three months, and out of curiosity, the past ten days. I get the information through <u>Standard and Poor</u>. I also use the Dow Jones retrieval system.

By using this analysis, I see that not only has it been volatile for the past 52 weeks, but that it has consistently been volatile for a long period of time, as well as a short period of time. Although I calculate it for ten days, taken alone, it's not really significant. Three months is important, as are the longer periods.

I usually find a strong relationship between the volatility in the 52 week period and the three month period. It's a check, a comparison with the other convertibles.

Compare one with the other and use this as a rating form.

We will look at all the convertibles and focus on those that meet our criteria. No doubt, we will eliminate many perhaps because the premiums are too large, or because the conversion value is too high, or because the volatility is too low. Look for the best, and make a short list. Before you actually invest, bring your information right up to date, using the current edition of the newspaper or by calling your broker.

Lesson 9
Exercise to Select the Top Profit-Taker Convertible

It is strongly recommended that you do this exercise before you invest. Use the sample convertibles in Figure 29. The highs and lows of the underlying stocks are given to you in Figure 30. Calculate the volatility of the underlying stocks from these figures and complete information on Figure 31. (Completed format and comments are on page 218 to 220). This is only a hypothetical exercise and should not be used in deciding current choices. Only the procedure should be used to select current Profit-Taker hedging situations.

Select the top convertible from the examples listed in Figure 29. Base your decision on the first five criteria of the Profit-Taker Checklist on page 206. But first, complete the "volatility column" in Figure 29. The "highs" and "lows" required to calculate the volatilities are in Figure 30. This is how we start to set up the Profit-Taker strategy. Remember when you are developing the short list, such as the one in Figure 29, start with the premium around 20 percent and under. I want you to check the market price and the conversion value. In addition, look for a conversion value of $1,000.00 or under. I don't mind if it's 1,010.00,

215

CONVER-TIBLE	PREMIUM(%)	CONVERSION VALUE(%)	VOLATILITY (52 WEEKS)	CURRENT YIELD(CONV.)	DIVIDENDS (STOCKS)
Alexanders Inc. 5-1/2% of 1996	9	79.46		6.3	Nil
Citicorp 5-3/4% of 2000	16	82.01		6.1	6.1
Dayco Corp. 6% of 1994	10	75.29		7.3	1.5
Dorchester Gas 8-1/2% of 2005	9	64.89		12.0	0.7
Federal National Mortgage Assn. 4-3/8% of 1996	6	75.78		5.5%	1.1
Ford Motor (Credit) 4-5/8% of 1998	3	83.70		5.2	4.6
Frontier Holdings (Air) 6% of 1992	8	76.29		7.3	1.9
Kaneb Services (Moran) 8-3/4% of 2008	8	86.93		9.4	6.8
Kuliche & Soffa 8% of 2008	14	99.71		7.0	0.4
Seagram Co. (J.E. Seagram) 8-1/4% of 2008	17	87.09		8.1	2.4

Figure 29. Exercise II: Selecting the Top Profit-Taker Convertibles

216

NAME OF CONVERTIBLE	HIGH	LOW	CLOSE
Alexanders Inc. 5-1/2% of 1996	28-1/2	13-1/4	25-5/8
Citicorp 5-3/4% of 2000	46-1/8	30-1/2	33-5/8
Dayco Corp. 6% of 1994	19-1/8	10-1/8	15-3/4
Dorchester Gas 8-1/2% of 2005	22-1/4	9-3/4	22-3/8
Federal National Mortgage Assn. 4-3/8% of 1996	30-1/8	12-1/8	14-7/8
Ford Motor (Credit) 4-5/8% of 1998	46-3/8	26	34-7/8
Frontier Holdings (Air) 6% of 1992	22-3/8	8-1/4	10-3/8
Kaneb Services (Moran) 8-3/4% of 2008	21-1/8	13-1/2	15-1/4
Kuliche & Soffa 8% of 2008	35-1/4	16-1/8	21-1/4
Seagram Co. (J.E. Seagram) 8-1/4% of 2008	40	27-1/4	32-7/8

Figure 30. Highs and Lows (52 Weeks)

217

but it should be around $1,000.00 or under. Also, I want you to be comfortable calculating volatility. It's critical you know where to get this information. Certainly, consider the yield of the bond as opposed to the dividend of the underlying stock. However, I cannot stress the importance of volatility strongly enough. This is where you make your real profit gains. The interest on the convertible is "nice to have". Now, choose the one best convertible from the short list in Figure 29.

In Figure 31 the convertibles are listed with the volatility information, but for practice, attempt to calculate the volatility percentages yourself first. The culminating choice is boxed, although the evaluation, once the criteria have been satisfied, is still somewhat subjective. Nevertheless, this structure takes most of the guess work out of the selection.

Results of Convertible Selection Exercise
(Figure 31)

Remember, these are our choices to start a half hedge. We know that volatility is critical. We want lots of action. The premiums are all well under 15 percent except for Seagram 8-1/4% of 2008. We said that we did not want anything over $1,000.00 (conversion value), and all the candidates met the criteria. That will be discussed in depth later. Kuliche & Soffa 8% of 2008 is exciting because of its high volatility: 90

218

percent. And Federal National Mortgages 4-3/8% of 1996 volatility at 121% is going to spoil you. You should not find anything that good so fast. Federal National Mortgages 4-3/8% of 1996 is truly exceptional! Frontier Holdings (Air) 6% of 1992 also has a great attraction because of its high volatility, but subsequently was pre-empted because of a low rating on fundamentals, primarily a high debt factor.

Dorchester Gas 8-1/2% of 2005 has, in the past, been a recommendation of mine. It has done very well, but the volatility at that time was much higher. The nice thing about Dorchester Gas is that if you wanted to use a 20 to 25 percent margin, the interest on the bond would pay a substantial part of the margin cost to your broker at the current rate. Of course, if you had a cash account, you would receive the full amount of the convertible interest. Nevertheless, volatility really settles the issue. It is so important!

We welcome action. It is through volatility that you can make money very quickly, regardless of whether the market goes up or down, because it's like "condensing time". These two bonds should be checked out very closely: Federal National Mortgage 4-3/8% of 1996 and Kuliche & Soffa 8% of 2008. The others do not appear to meet our guidelines. Very probably, they will not provide enough action.

CONVER-TIBLE	PREMIUM(%)	CONVERSION VALUE(%)	VOLATILITY (52 WEEKS)	CURRENT YIELD(CONV.)	DIVIDENDS (STOCKS)
Alexanders Inc. 5-1/2% of 1996	9	79.46	59.51	6.3	Nil
Citicorp 5-3/4% of 2000	16	82.01	46.47	6.1	6.1
Dayco Corp. 6% of 1994	10	75.29	57.14	7.3	1.5
Dorchester Gas 8-1/2% of 2005	9	64.89	55.86	12.0	0.7
Federal National Mortgage Assn. 4-3/8% of 1996	6	75.78	121.01	5.5%	1.1
Ford Motor (Credit) 4-5/8% of 1998	3	83.70	58.42	5.2	4.6
Frontier Holdings (Air) 6% of 1992	8	76.29	136.14	7.3	1.9
Kaneb Services (Moran) 8-3/4% of 2008	8	86.93	50.00	9.4	6.8
Kuliche & Soffa 8% of 2008	14	99.71	90.00	7.0	0.4
Seagram Co. (J.E. Seagram) 8-1/4% of 2008	17	87.09	38.75	8.1	2.4

Figure 31. Completed Volatility Percentages

220

We will now consider something I have not mentioned, which is the "Call Price" listed under Column 15 in Value Line (Figure 12, pages 144 and 145). Call Price is something that corporations love. In a way, it is good for us as investors, as well. The call price is written into the original charter of the bond or the convertible preferred. For example, Avnet Inc. 8% of 2013 has a call price of 103.20. This means that if the corporation so wishes, it can call in and pay off their bond before the maturity date and confer a bonus over the $1,000.00. The bonus they would be obliged to pay is $32.00 per bond.

This is what happens in real life. Most of the time the corporation is not interested in settling the debt early. However, take a situation where you have a particular convertible bond and the stock goes up. The call price is $1,050.00. Because your bond is tied to the stock, it goes up to $1,500.00 (and you can convert it into $1,500.00 worth of common stock). The corporation would say this would be a good time to pay $1,050.00 for that issue because the bond is worth $1,500.00, and so they decide to call in the bonds.

Normally, the corporation has to give at least sixty days notice to creditors if they are going to call in the bonds. If you are holding that bond, you will be advised very quickly. They

221

know that the bond is worth $1,500.00 of common stock. Now put yourself in the picture. You purchased that bond when the conversion value was under $1,000.00; now it is worth $1,500.00 of common stock. The corporation announces they are calling in the issue. No one in their right mind is going to accept $1,050.00 when it is worth $1,500.00.

Furthermore, they <u>want</u> you to convert it, and obviously you will convert it into common stock before the due date. They are elated with that because they have eliminated their respective debt. As you can see, in this situation they have eliminated their debt because you have converted into common stock. This has diluted the corporation's stock somewhat, but in a strong bull market the dilution is looked after very quickly.

The corporation would never call their bonds in when it is very close to the call price because, within sixty days, the price might go down and they would still be obliged to pay the call price. Why would they want to pay it when there is a chance of eliminating the debt if the stock goes up? My experience has been that the bond price is well over the call price before the corporation considers a call.

We never buy when the convertible bond is well over $1,000.00 (conversion value), do we? If the corporation does call in the bonds, any premium that exists, usually disappears completely. The bond here is normally only worth what the stock is worth. Another reason I have implemented the "under $1,000.00" criterion is so that you will never be in an unprofitable situation should the corporation decide to call their issues in. It is most unlikely that they will call it in below the call price.

There are two reasons why we buy when the conversion value is under $1,000.00. First, this is the area where it generally holds up if the stock goes down. The second reason, which is just as important, is in case it goes up and is called. By the way, corporations do not always call in the bond simply because the conversion value rises above the call price. Prices for convertibles may rise to well over $2,000.00. Also, if general interest rates are low, the corporation may leave an advantageous financial arrangement alone.

Using the criteria you are learning here, you should never be in an unprofitable situation if the bonds are called in. If it does happen, the interest is paid up to date. If you buy a bond, you pay the accrued interest up to the date of the purchase. When you sell the bond, you collect the interest up to the date of the sale.

Getting back to Kuliche & Soffa 8% of 2008, although the call price is $1,069.00. I wouldn't worry about that. It will be well above that before they call it in.

I go over all the bonds every month, both American and Canadian. The American bonds are nicely set out for us, and it is easy to look at them quickly. But don't overlook the Canadian market. Every once in a while there is a great one. When my choice has been Canadian, it has done exceedingly well.

If your selection becomes less volatile over a period of time, you might consider switching that plan for another. As your portfolio gets larger, I strongly recommend that you diversify, that you have more than one plan going. I have had as many as eighteen or nineteen plans active at one time. Each one is a little bit different. That way you don't get bored. There is always action.

There are a couple of important points that must be mentioned at this time. Investors sometimes ask about negative premiums that they come across in Value Line (i.e., those that have a minus sign in front of them). When I first saw negative premiums, I thought I had stumbled on the panacea to instant investment success. I thought I would make a vast amount of money, because that negative premium means your common stock would be worth more than the convertible bond. You would simply buy the convertible, convert it into common stock, sell the stock in order to produce the self-evident profit. Alas, the real truth is that market prices are not exact in time. You might set out to get a zero or a negative premium, but there may have been many trades of the bond or the stock that day, at different times. Consequently, the prices would probably change accordingly when you wanted to buy. If you do get a negative premium, accept it graciously as a bonus. However, do not forget that your commissions are absorbing one to three percent.

Another point. When you are looking up a stock in the financial pages, you will sometimes see two or three or more issues of the same corporation listed. The first one, the common stock, is normally the one you are interested in. There is only one common stock for a corporation. The others are the preferred, and are not the stock for which the convertible bond can be exchanged, unless otherwise stated.

Lesson 10
<u>The Profit-Taker Strategy</u>

The half hedge can be very lucrative, but let me tell you what I found somewhat discouraging. Like most people, I had two targets, one long term goal if it went up, and one long term goal if it went down.

It is much like romance. It it went up one day, I was elated. If it went down, I was despondent. The price went back and forth, but I wasn't making anything from these fluctuations. I felt I was doing something wrong. I was not gaining anything from all the fluctuations in between my unyielding long term goals.

Even if you are in a profitable situation one day, when you are down the next day, you are no further ahead, are you? Not until you make a decision to take your profits.

It occurred to me that I was trying to take every dollar out of the market rather than the profits as they occurred. Fortunately, over time, I developed a disciplined, protective, and profitable technique. I'll now reveal it to you.

Instead of having one long term goal on the upside, and one long term goal on the downside, it seemed to me it might be a much better idea to have sub-goals on the upside and downside, and lock in gains from the many fluctuations. That way I would take a number of smaller profits rather than hope for the "jackpot", which often never happens. So I tried this plan.

Now, I would like to go back to the Rob M Blind stock situation as an example for setting up a Profit-Taker strategy. Let's do a Profit-Taker strategy from the beginning. To refresh your memory, the bond is selling at $900.00. The stock is selling at $30.00 each. Each bond is exchangeable into 30 shares. There is no premium. You should now have a good grasp of these selection criteria.

Now we'll set up a half hedge. That is, we'll order 10 bonds of Rob M Blind Corporation. Our broker phones us and confirms the order has been filled. You normally use a half hedge to start the Profit-Taker strategy. (Figure 32).

That means selling short 150 shares (half of our 300 shares). Now you have bought your 10 bonds, you have sold short half of the underlying stock represented by the convertibles (150 shares). You can use a form similar to the one in Figure 33 to help you set up your plan.

The price we paid (purchase price) was $30.00 per share. Set up two long term goals,

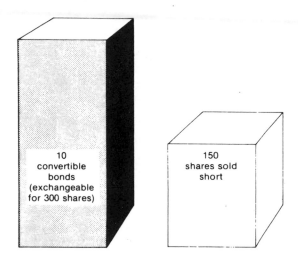

Figure 32. The Start of the Abrams Automatic
Profit-Taker

one on the upside, which, for the purpose of our example, is $60.00. On the downside it will be a very conservative zero. Simply divide these long term goals into three equal sub-goals. On the upside: 40, 50, and 60. On the downside: 20, 10, and 0. (Figure 33).

By the way, it's important to note that when the final long term goal on the upside is reached, you have, in effect, a full hedge. You end up with 300 shares sold short, which is the long term goal. On the downside, you will end up with zero, to satisfy the long term goal, with no short sales left. In other words, for practical purposes, the full hedge at the top is the end of your plan, and happens when the number of shares sold short equals the number of shares represented by your bond (10 bonds = 300 shares). Now, simply divide your stock into three equal parts to determine your sub-goals. You will have three equal parts on the upside and three equal parts on the downside. This will give you the balance that we have discussed. We make transactions at each sub-goal.

Remember, with this strategy, always sell short when the stock moves up, and when the stock moves down, always buy in or cover. Now we have a series of small hedges.

The initial stock price is $30.00. No one knows which way the stock is going to move.

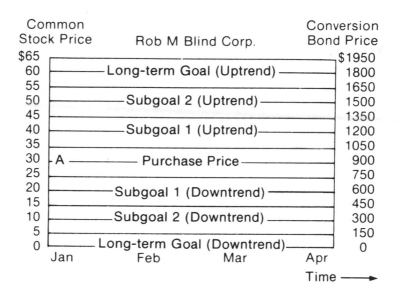

Figure 33. Setting the Goals for the Abrams
Automatic Profit-Taker

You are in a beautiful position because you have made the decision as to what to do if the stock moves up or down. The plan is set; you phone your broker and place two open orders (also called advance orders, or good-until cancelled orders). They work very efficiently.

Your broker takes your order and he relays it to the selling floor, where the traders there fill it as soon as the prices come up. I am sure that you will not be able to resist following along regularly in the newspaper or through a computer service.

Your initial advance order in our example is as follows: sell short 50 shares at $40.00 if the stock moves up. If this order were filled, you would have a balance of 200 shares sold short. If the stock goes down, you want to cover 50 shares at $20.00. In this case, you would have a balance left of 100 shares sold short. You do not, of course, know which way it is going to move.

For instance, if the stock happens to move up, it triggers your order at the first sub-goal. Your broker calls you and announces that your order to sell short 50 shares at $40.00 has been filled. What are you going to do next?

First, cancel all previous orders so as not to have any future confusion with the plan.

Now, place your next two orders. First, sell short 50 shares at $50.00, and that will give you a balance of 250 shares sold short, if required. Secondly, if the stock goes down, you want to cover 50 shares at $30.00, and then you will be right back where you started with 150 shares sold short.

This time the stock happens to move back down. It triggers the order at $30.00. Your broker phones you and informs you that the order has been filled. Ordinarily, you would be right back where you started, back at $30.00, and you would have accomplished nothing.

But because you have a structure or plan, you now have the ability to lock in a profit. You sold short 50 shares at $40.00. With this short sale, if the price moves down, as it did, that will be profitable for you.

When it went from $40.00 to $30.00, you made 50 shares times $10.00, or $500.00. And that is true whenever there is any fluctuation between two sub-goals.

You are making a profit here because you had the foresight to sell 50 shares at $40.00. When it fell from $40.00 to $30.00, with a $10.00 decline, you had 50 shares to sell short and they were covered for a gain of $10.00 per share or a total of $500.00. (See Figure 34).

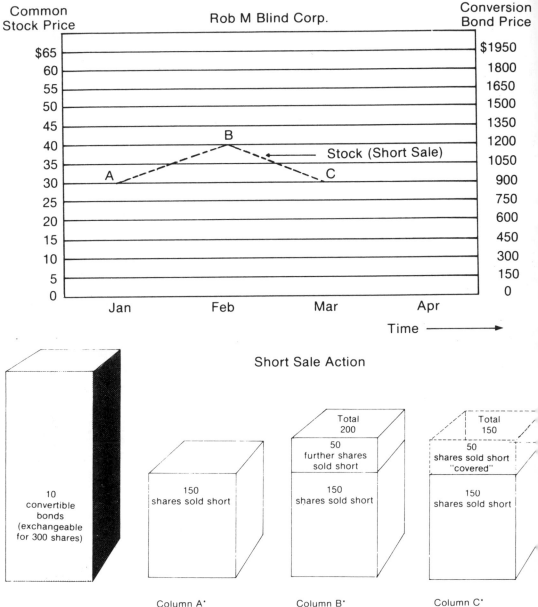

*Columns A, B and C apply to the corresponding letters on the price graph above

Important: The number of convertible bonds remains the same through the entire action, therefore the number of shares the convertible bonds represent remains constant. Only the number of shares sold short fluctuates.

Figure 34. The Abrams Automatic Profit-Taker in Action
Uptrend Fluctuations in Price

Is there a problem selling short 50 stocks at a time rather than blocks of 100? Although 100 shares is a round lot, and anything under 100 shares is an odd lot, this is seldom a problem today. In fact, sometimes it is easier to get odd lots. Don't concern yourself too much with odd lots, and thereby lose a profit.

To be perfectly clear, let's take another example. Now, start again. Start with 150 shares sold short as before, but this time we will look at it from a different angle. The 150 shares were sold short at $30.00. Everybody agrees we do not know which way the stock is going to move.

Let's review. What is the first order? Sell short 50 shares at $40.00. What is the second order? Cover 50 shares at $20.00. This time the stock goes down and triggers the order at $20.00. The broker calls and says that the order on the downside has been filled. Here is what you have done. You covered 50 of the 150 shares sold short and you now have a balance of 100 shares sold short. You made money when it went down. It declined $10.00 and you took $500.00 profit from the short sale.

The next comment to your broker should be, "clear the board, cancel all previous orders". Always do this when you have an order filled. Put in two new orders for your next immediate goal on the upside, and for your next immediate goal on the downside. You give your broker the order in advance, telling him what to do if the stock goes up, and what to do if the stock goes down. Your broker will advise you when your order has been filled.

Next, the price of the stock moves up and triggers your order at $30.00. You are right back where you started. Or are you? There is one exciting difference: you have a profit of $500.00 because you covered 50 shares that went from $30.00 to $20.00. Place your orders again. (Figure 35).

When you use the Abrams Automatic Profit-Taker, you lock in profits. You are making money on the upside because you have 150 shares not covered by the short sale. 150 shares were sold short at the start of the strategy and this left 150 shares outstanding. These outstanding shares guarantee you a profit on the upside. The 150 shares sold should produce gains on the downside.

You have taken a $500.00 profit here on each small fluctuation, that is, $500.00 of the realized $1,500.00 on the upside. But you are still left with 100 shares open for more profit if the stock continues to advance.

Can relatively minor fluctuations produce

Price Action

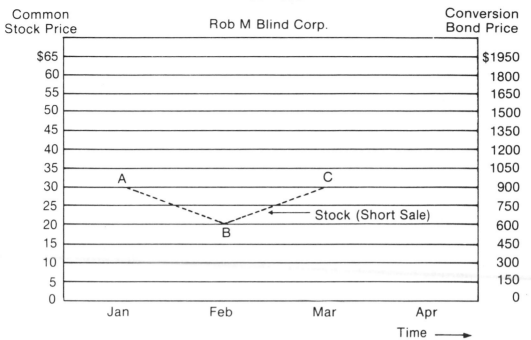

Short Sale Action

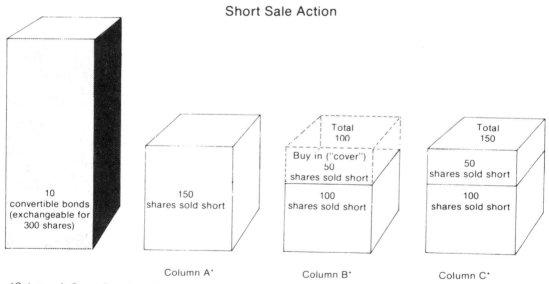

Column A*

Column B*

Column C*

*Columns A, B and C apply to the corresponding letters on the price graph above

Important: The number of convertible bonds remains the same throughout the entire action, therefore the number of shares the convertible bonds represent remains constant. Only the number of shares sold short fluctuates.

Figure 35. The Abrams Automatic Profit-Taker in Action

Downtrend Fluctuations in Price

gains at any stage of the upside or downside trend? Gains will be generated whenever the common stock bounces between any two of our sub-goals, resulting in the filling of our previously placed orders. Each time the stock fluctuates between sub-goals, it automatically scores for us.

This is profitable when it seesaws between any two sub-goals on an uptrend such as between $40.00 and $50.00. (Figure 36).

The fluctuations are correspondingly profitable when they bounce between sub-goals on a downtrend, such as between $20.00 and $10.00. (Figure 37).

There is absolutely no limit to the number of times it may shuttle between your sub-goals, each time putting more money into your account, well before your long term goals are met.

There are, of course, an almost unlimited number of combinations of fluctuations that the movement of common stock might form; however, the same profitable concept applies.

It is imperative that you select securities whose market prices are "lively" or volatile in nature, as the faster the common stock moves, the larger your profits are likely to be, and in

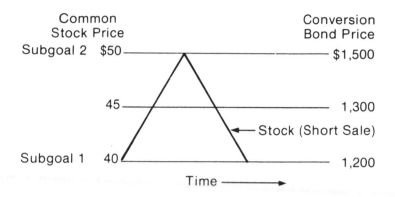

Figure 36. Fluctuation Between Two Subgoals on an Uptrend

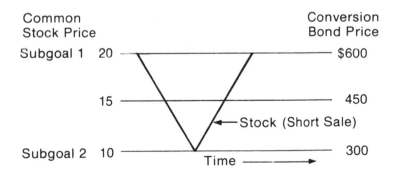

Figure 37. Fluctuation Between Two Subgoals on a Downtrend

less time. If your plan should have an unlikely run on the upside without fluctuating between your sub-goals, that is, it reaches Sub-goal 1 ($40.00), advances to Sub-goal 2 ($50.00) and then concludes by filling your order at the Long-term Goal ($60.00), you would have a total gain of $3000.00. To further detail the case in point:

Sub-goal 1 $500.00 gain on shares represented by convertibles. 'Locked-in' by selling short 50 shares X $10 gain.

Sub-goal 2 $1000.00 gain on shares represented by convertibles. 'Locked-in' by selling short 50 shares X $20 gain.

Sub-goal 3 $1500.00 gain on shares represented by convertibles. 'Locked-in' by selling short remaining 50 shares X $30 gain.

Thus the total gain is $3000.00

Conversely, if your plan should have an improbable straight run on the downside without fluctuating between your sub-goals, the outcome would be calculated by the short sale in concert with the downward resistant senior status of the convertible. (Personally, I have inadvertently had a hedged windfall when the corporation with which I was hedging went bankrupt. I not only gained from the short sale, but also the senior convertible issue which was subsequently paid in full, that is, $1000.00 par value per convertible bond, as part of the debt obligation by the take-over company).

Try one yourself. Remember, the plan ends in a full hedge on the upside. When you set the plan up and buy the convertibles, that's a debit and when you sell short, that is listed as a credit. The reverse is true when you cover your short sale and sell or convert your bonds.

When you have reached 300 shares sold short, you now have a full hedge, and this is normally the end of your plan. When it is a full hedge, you have locked in all the profits. <u>You</u> do not decide when this will happen, the <u>stock</u> decides how much profit you are going to make.

After you have realized your planned profits and you wish to convert your bonds, there are no commissions to be paid. It is one of the few free things in the stock market. There is an assumption that you always have to pay commissions to sell stock, but here you have already sold the stock short. When you convert these 10 bonds, how many stocks do you receive? The answer is 300. You have previously already sold 300, so they offset each other. Sound a little complex? It's one of those things that is easier to do than to explain.

I want to say a couple of things about this. You do not collect the accumulated interest when you convert, so check the interest rate, and if it's coming up in the next few weeks, you might as well collect the interest before you convert.

Also, wait a while in case the stock goes back down. I would like it to go back down because, in our example, I would then put an order in to cover 50 shares at $50.00. If it does trigger the sub-goal on the downside, the action starts over again. The profits would continue on. If the stock advances to well over $60.00 or $65.00, then I assume that the plan is over and I would terminate it, of course. The more fluctuations you have, the greater the profits. Each one of these steps is a hedge of its own.

Is the downside goal always "0"? Yes. Sometimes people who flourish with this strategy rationalize that "0" is unrealistic. Stocks rarely ever go to "0", they say, so they start setting arbitrary downside long-term goals. There is a problem with this, and there is an advantage to leaving it at "0".

When you make the long-term "0", you always have some short sales left, unless the price goes to "0". At one time, I set an arbitrary downside long-term goal at 15, which I thought would never be reached.

In the stock market, the unpredictable often happens. The stock did fall below the $15.00 mark. Consequently, I had no shares to sell short. That meant that I had all the naked bonds and all the short sales were covered.

With the "0" goal, if it should drop to sub-goal 2, you have an option. If it's volatile, let it go. No problem for you here. If it slows down, you may be in a very profitable position with a large premium. If the bond has resisted the downtrend, you may decide to sell your bonds, cover the remainder of your short sale, take your profit, and start another plan. You have a choice. But if you do not keep "0" as your long-term goal, and you run out of short sales, you do not have this choice.

Allow me to say a word about the upside. I put $60.00 as the long term-goal as an example, but in actual fact, I often close that up considerably so that I get more action. I often make my long term goal approximately 45 percent (plus premium) of the current purchase price. In other words, it would be around $43.50. 60 percent is very conservative on the upside. Usually 45 percent gives you a lot of action between your sub-goals. Take into account the need to produce a substantial profit after deducting any commissions and expenses.

How many bonds do you have to buy? I

suggest a minimum of three to set up a strategy. So if you're paying, say $900.00, three bonds would be $2,700.00 and you would be responsible for 25 percent of $2,700.00. You would put up about $700.00 to $800.00 if you're on full margin.

Buy at least three bonds so you are making good use of your commissions. The small investor nearly always has a big disadvantage with commissions, so the more volume you have, the better. As long as you remember to judge your goals accordingly. If the price of the stock is low, say below $10.00, you are going to get a lot more stock and, consequently, it is much easier to buy in round lots. But again, do not be overly concerned about odd lots.

How long will one of the Profit-Taker plans last? The longest plan I have held is approximately 2-1/2 years. Sometimes they last 3 months. The shortest was 6 weeks. I have had to wait sometimes 3 months to have one sub-goal filled. On the other hand, I've had two orders filled on the same day. What I am saying is this: do not expect it to happen uniformly. It doesn't work that way. It can be very erratic. What is important is the average over 6 months to a year, to evaluate how well it performs.

As soon as you feel comfortable with this

strategy, have three, or four, or five plans going at the same time. I cannot imagine a more conservative way of going about investing. As practice, I suggest you follow one theoretically in the newspaper. Or go back six months and follow through on our procedure and find out how well you would have done had you followed the system. Compare the results with whatever else you are doing. You may be elated!

If you are inclined to set up more than one Profit-Taker plan initially, consider making your selection over a period of time - perhaps implementing one plan per month. This arrangement will allow you a cross section of the best opportunities that occur over a longer period of time.

What happens if your order is filled at a better price than the advance order you originally placed? It happens. Accept it graciously. I used to adjust my plan if I had a better fill than I placed. Now I just accept it and enjoy it. There is always that chance that they will fill it at a better price. Fortunately, they can't fill it at a worse price.

What happens if a broker misses filling an order? I know investors worry about that at first, but it very seldom happens. You can follow along in the newspaper. If you put an order in and you see in the paper that someone else has an order filled at a better price than you (even 1/8th of a point better), the investment house has an obligation to fill your order at that price. When your broker places your order, each request is recorded. When your order comes up, it is filled. When you put the order in advance, you get priority over someone who put their order in at the same price at a later time.

Lesson 11
<u>Selecting a Broker and a Final Comment</u>

I want to say a few words about how to select a broker. First of all, do not make the mistake made by so many investors, by selecting an investment house because it predicts the future. Investment houses don't know! I want to urge you to look for a broker who doesn't try to predict which way the market is going to move. What you want is a knowledgeable broker who is going to give you the best information that you need to ride the fluctuations. You want good service. You want a broker who phones you promptly when an order is filled. When they learn that they get two more orders every time an order is filled, quite frankly, you won't have any trouble from then on.

Sometimes I have found that there was resistance by some investment houses and by some brokers toward helping investors set up a Profit-Taker strategy. There is a reason for this. They do not always feel confident if they haven't done it before. Being human, they want a comfortable niche. They often concentrate on what their research department recommends. And do not forget, they get good commissions for buying and selling common stock, much higher commissions than convertible bonds. But they

247

also do well with you. With the short sale, you pay commissions. (But you do not put up any further investment money for that short sale). Do not hesitate to let your broker know that you expect prompt service and assistance with hedging information.

You want a broker who is knowledgeable and ambitious. Do not hesitate to visit two or three brokers. When your car needs a major repair or body work, you go to more than one mechanic. Often people do that with brokers. If you do not know anybody at an investment house, ask for the sales manager. Tell him you are interested in hedging and ask him to recommend someone to speak with, someone in the office who might be familiar with the area of hedging, such as described here in The Profit-Taker Breakthrough.

Ask questions like, "what are the margin requirements for convertible bonds?" It should be around 20 to 25 percent of the market price. Ask them if they have any problem implementing short sales on the U.S. or Canadian market. There should be no problem with that.

Ask them what their minimum commission is. It should be something like $30.00 to $45.00 at a discount broker, $75.00 at a full-service broker. Ask if there is interest paid on the balance of your account that you do not have invested. If you have unused money in your account, many investment houses pay you interest on the outstanding balance. It varies among investment houses, for example, sometimes there has to be a balance of over $1,000.00. Check with your broker. It is important that you have a knowledgeable individual within the investment house that is most advantageous to you.

No doubt, you have asked yourself: "What's wrong with this strategy?" There has to be something wrong with everything. Have you ever noticed that there are few things perfect in this world? If there is anything wrong with this strategy, it is that it makes people too confident. I knew one investor who had been very successful with the system and he looked back at it and said that if he had not made that short sale, he would have made even more. So he went back to his old ways and tried to predict which way the market was going to move, only to fail. Don't fall into the trap of overconfidence.

Another concern is that there might be times when the bond will fall at the same rate as the short sale without forming a premium immediately. That can create a temporary loss situation. But it is nice to know that it is temporary.

Aren't you afraid that everyone will do this and decrease the opportunities? Remember, a lot of people are not willing to take the time to read a book or come to a seminar, and those who do, do not always use this strategy. Often they revert back to trying to predict. There are always people who will try to guess which way the market will move, and they will ultimately lose money. We know that corporations appreciate convertible bonds. As they become more popular, new convertibles will be issued, which will create greater opportunities for us.

Now let's summarize the steps to implement a Profit-Taker Plan. (Figure 38). So, select your broker. Be sure he or she is familiar with hedging in the U.S. and preferably in the Canadian market as well. If you are taking positions with both U.S. and Canadian convertibles, ask your broker to maintain a separate margin account for each. That way you can save your fees from constantly transferring U.S. to Canadian funds or vice versa. Allow the funds in each account to accumulate until you are ready to take your profits. You are not in the business here of making a profit resulting from the differences in currency prices.

Select your bonds the way I have showed you in the previous chapters. Get your short list. Apply the Checklist (Figure 28) as we did in Lesson 9 to the short list. Obtain the most recent information from the United States and Canadian financial newspapers, or from your broker. Find out exactly what the premium is and the conversion value. It may well have worked in your favour. Before you do anything, be sure to inquire about the short sale with your broker. Does he see a problem with the short sale?

The first thing you do is place your order for the bonds at the price that you want. Limit it to one day because the stock prices can change over a couple of days.

Tell your broker the price you want to pay for that convertible. If you do not get that price, just reassess your situation and put your order in again. Make it a price that will please you. You will most likely get it somewhere between the BID and ASK. Do not leave the price to the discretion of the trading floor. When the bond order is filled, do not fool around trying to predict which way the stock price is going to move before placing your short sale order.

Put your short sale for the Profit-Taker Hedge at the current market price. Place your order in to sell short one half of the shares the bond represents. When that order is filled, you are in business.

You set up your long term goals exactly as we did in the example. Divide your shares into three equal parts for your short term goals. Call your broker and put in two open orders: one on the upside to sell short, and one on the downside to cover.

Some people ask me, "won't this strategy take a lot of time?" I say, not as much time as laying awake wondering what is going to happen the next day. Once you set up a plan, the decisions are made, and it will be automatic. Once it starts making money for you, you will not be able to resist calling your broker. It may be the most satisfying call of the day.

<u>STEPS TO IMPLEMENTATION</u>

1. SELECT BROKER (N.Y., AMEX)

2. SET UP MARGIN ACCOUNT(S)

3. PRE-SELECT BONDS

4. APPLY CHECKLIST

5. OBTAIN PRICES:
    - BROKER
    - SUNDAY N.Y. TIMES, BARRON'S
6. SHORT SALES AVAILABLE:
    - BOARD LOTS
    - ODD LOTS
7. SELECT BONDS

8. PLACE ORDER FOR BONDS; LIMIT ONE DAY

9. MARKET ORDER (SHORT SELL)

10. SET LONG-TERM GOALS

11. SET SHORT-TERM GOALS

12. PLACE TWO OPEN ORDERS (SUB-GOALS)

Figure 38

APPENDIX 1

EXAMPLE OF FULL HEDGE:

ANNUALIZED RETURN OF 117.3%

FEDERAL INDUSTRIES
8% OF 2006
(DETAILS FOLLOW)

CONVERTIBLE FULL HEDGE WORKSHEET

COMPANY: Federal Industries 8% 15JUN06

Acquisition

Buy.....................$10,000 @ $86.00 − $8,600.00
Convertible Bonds

Sell Short...............$540 @ $13.25 = $(6,965.29)
Common Stock

Total Capital Invested........................**$1,634.71**

Total Interest Earned on Bond............$1,078.36

Total Borrowing Charges Paid.................$139.20
($8.70 X 16 months)

Total Dividends Paid on Short...............$108.00
 Position

Total Net Income................................**$831.16**

CONVERTIBLE FULL HEDGE WORKSHEET

COMPANY: Federal Industries 8% 15JUN06

Disposal

Sell......................$10,000 @ $83.00 = $8,300.00
Convertible Bonds

Cover Short.............$540 @ $9.148 = $(4,939.92)
Common Stock

Total Capital Invested........................$1,634.71

Net Proceeds from unwind.................**$1,160.08**

Total Net Capital Gain/Loss................$1,725.37

Total Net Income (interest only)..............$831.16

Annual Yield (interest only).......................38.%

Total Return...**156.3%**
(Interest + Capital Gain/Loss over 16 mths)

ANNUALIZED RETURN:.........................**117.3%**

Source: Available upon request.

APPENDIX 2

EXAMPLE OF FULL HEDGE:

ANNUALIZED RETURN OF 67.3%

CONNOR PERIPHERALS
6.5% OF 2002
(DETAILS FOLLOW)

CONVERTIBLE FULL HEDGE WORKSHEET

COMPANY: Connor Peripherals 6.5%
01MAR02

Acquisition

Buy..................$10,000 @ $113.00 = $11,300.00
Convertible Bonds

Sell Short...............$417 @ $21.69 = $(9,044.73)
Common Stock

Total Capital Invested........................**$2,255.27**

Total Interest Earned on Bond...............$399.00

Total Borrowing Charges Paid.................$113.05
($16.15 X 7 months)

Total Dividends Paid on Short........................$0
 Position

Total Net Income................................**$285.95**

CONVERTIBLE FULL HEDGE WORKSHEET

COMPANY: Connor Peripherals 6.5%
01MAR02

Disposal

Sell......................$10,000 @ $86.45 = $8,645.00
Convertible Bonds

Cover Short..............417 @ $13.88 = $(5,785.88)
Common Stock

Total Capital Invested........................$2,255.27

Net Proceeds from unwind.................**$2,859.12**

Total Net Capital Gain/Loss...................$603.85

Total Net Income (interest only).............$285.95

Annual Yield (interest only)....................21.73%

Total Return.......................................**39.45%**
(Interest + Capital Gain/Loss over 16 mths)

ANNUALIZED RETURN:........................**67.3%**

Source: Available upon request.

APPENDIX 3

EXAMPLE OF FULL HEDGE:

ANNUALIZED RETURN OF 32.13%

PWA
7.625% of 1996
(DETAILS FOLLOW)

CONVERTIBLE FULL HEDGE WORKSHEET

COMPANY: PWA 7.625% 30DEC96

Acquisition

Buy.................$10,000 @ $103.33 = $10,333.30
Convertible Bonds

Sell Short.............$416 @ $19.008 = $(7,907.33)
Common Stock

Total Capital Invested.......................**$2,425.97**

Total Interest Earned on Bond............$1,408.22

Total Borrowing Charges Paid................$217.36
($9.88 X 22 months)

Total Dividends Paid on Short.......................$0
 Position

Total Net Income...........................**$1,190.86**

CONVERTIBLE FULL HEDGE WORKSHEET

COMPANY: PWA 7.625% 30DEC96

Disposal

Sell........................$10,000 @ $75.00 = $7,500.00
Convertible Bonds

Cover Short...........$416 @ $11.625 = $(4,836.00)
Common Stock

Total Capital Invested........................$2,425.97

Net Proceeds from unwind.................**$2,664.00**

Total Net Capital Gain/Loss...................$238.03

Total Net Income (interest only)...........$1,190.86

Annual Yield (interest only).....................26.7%

Total Return...**58.9%**
(Interest + Capital Gain/Loss over 16 mths)

ANNUALIZED RETURN:........................**32.13%**

Source: Available upon request.

APPENDIX 4

EXAMPLE OF FULL HEDGE:

ANNUALIZED RETURN OF 36.4%

WABAN
6.5% Of 2002
(DETAILS FOLLOW)

CONVERTIBLE FULL HEDGE WORKSHEET

COMPANY: Waban 6.5% 01JUL02

<u>Acquisition</u>

Buy.....................$10,000 @ $97.30 =   9,730.00
Convertible Bonds

Sell Short...............$404 @ $18.38 = <u>$(7,425.92)</u>
Common Stock

Total Capital Invested.......................**$2,304.08**

Total Interest Earned on Bond...............$975.00

Total Borrowing Charges Paid................$167.08
($9.28 X 18 months)

Total Dividends Paid on Short.......................$<u>0</u>
 Position

Total Net Income...............................**$807.92**

CONVERTIBLE FULL HEDGE WORKSHEET

COMPANY: Waban 6.5% 01JUL02

Disposal

Sell.....................$10,000 @ $91.00 = $9,100.00
Convertible Bonds

Cover Short.............$404 @ $15.71 = $(6,345.83)
Common Stock

Total Capital Invested........................$2,304.08

Net Proceeds from unwind.................**$2,754.17**

Total Net Capital Gain/Loss...................$450.09

Total Net Income (interest only).............$807.92

Annual Yield (interest only).....................23.3%

Total Return..**54.5%**
(Interest + Capital Gain/Loss over 16 mths)

ANNUALIZED RETURN:........................**36.4%**

Source: Available upon request.

APPENDIX 5

EXAMPLE OF FULL HEDGE:

ANNUALIZED RETURN OF 30.79%

ALBERTA ENERGY
6.75% of 2002
(DETAILS FOLLOW)

CONVERTIBLE FULL HEDGE WORKSHEET

COMPANY: Alberta Energy 6.75% 30JUN02

Acquisition

Buy......................$10,000 @ $95.00 = $9,500.00
Convertible Bonds

Sell Short................$427 @ $17.60 = $(7,518.31)
Common Stock

Total Capital Invested........................**$1,981.69**

Total Interest Earned on Bond.............$1,731.88

Total Borrowing Charges Paid.................$300.80
($9.40 X 32 months)

Total Dividends Paid on Short...............$281.82
  Position

Total Net Income..............................**$1,149.26**

CONVERTIBLE FULL HEDGE WORKSHEET

COMPANY: Alberta Energy 6.75% 30JUN02

Disposal

Sell......................$10,000 @ $75.93 = $7,593.00
Convertible Bonds

Cover Short.............$427 @ $12.02 = $(5,134.03)
Common Stock

Total Capital Invested........................$1,981.69

Net Proceeds from unwind..................**$2,458.97**

Total Net Capital Gain/Loss...................$477.28

Total Net Income (interest only)...........$1,149.26

Annual Yield (interest only).....................21.7%

Total Return...82.0%
(Interest + Capital Gain/Loss over 16 mths)

ANNUALIZED RETURN:.......................30.79%

Source: Available upon request.

Glossary of Key Terms as Applied to the Profit-Taker Concept

ARBITRAGE: buying an item and simultaneously selling another item into which the first is convertible. For example, a bond might be convertible into a fixed number of shares of common stock. If, for any reason, the bond price becomes less than the conversion value of the underlying common stock, a profit can be made (i) buying the bond and selling short the stock at the same time, (ii) converting the bond into the stock, and (iii) delivering the stock to cover the short sale. Arbitraging is carried on by professionals who are usually owners of stock exchange seats.

CALL PRICE: the price [in $ for convertible preferred; % of par ($1,000) for convertible bonds] at which the issue may be called for redemption. As a rule, the corporation agrees to give sixty days notice or more to the holder of the bond or preferred stock that is being called or redeemed.

CONVERSION VALUE (%): the value of the underlying common stock that could be realized through immediate conversion of the convertible bond expressed as a percentage. Preferred convertibles are quoted in dollars.

CURRENT YIELD (%): based on the interest rate included in the name of the convertible bond or the indicated annual dividend in the name of the convertible preferred. Both indicated as a percentage.

EXCHANGE: the exchange where the convertible security or underlying common stock trades. Although the convertible security and the common stock it represents usually are listed on the same exchange, it is not necessarily the case.

FULL HEDGE: a hedge which combines equal numbers of common stock into which a convertible security is exchangeable with stock sold short. (Number of common stock represented by convertible securities = the number of short sales).

HALF HEDGE: a hedge which combines the total number of common stock into which a convertible security is exchangeable with one-half of the stock sold short. (Number of common stock represented by the convertible securities = one-half of the number of short sales).

HEDGE: the reduction or elimination of the risk of an investment by adopting a protective strategy or making a transaction in another offsetting vehicle.

LEVERAGE: the intensified speculative effect of market fluctuations on a security through the use of "borrowed" money.

MATURITY: the date on which the convertible matures.

NO. OF SHARES: the number of common shares obtainable upon conversion.

PAYMENT DATES: for bonds refers to the dates on which the interest is paid, normally every six months. For preferreds, refers to the dates on which the dividends are paid.

PREMIUM: the difference between the price of the convertible and its conversion value, expressed as a percentage of the current market price of the securities obtainable upon conversion. The formula is:

$$\text{Premium}(\%) = \frac{\text{Convertible Price(\$) minus Conversion Value(\$)}}{\text{Conversion Value(\$)}} \times 100$$

PROFIT-TAKER CHECKLIST: a list of criteria to ensure your success with the Profit-Taker concept. Explained in Book III, Lesson 8 of The Profit-Taker Breakthrough.

THE PROFIT-TAKER HEDGE: an investment strategy that reduces or eliminates the risk of an investment by adopting a protective strategy or making a transaction in another offsetting vehicle. A characteristic of the Profit-Taker Hedge is that profits are made on relatively small fluctuations, regardless of the direction of the market.

PROGRAM TRADING: a hedge for large institutions and big investors to earn profits on small differences that develop between stock prices and related synergistic instruments such as future indexes.

SPREAD: in arbitrage transactions, the difference between the price of the same security, currency, or commodity in one market and the price in another.

VOLATILITY (%) (52 weeks): the price action of the underlying common stock based on 52 week's "high" and "low" expressed as a percentage of the current market price. The formula is:

$$\frac{\text{Hi minus Lo}}{\text{Current Market Price (Common Stock)}} \times 100$$

Volatility for the period of "last 12 weeks" and "previous 10 days" calculated in the same manner.

Don Abrams

Don Abrams embodies the philosophy that investing should be worry-free, "fun" and very profitable. He delivers his "fashionable" flair to finance with princely results. Graduating from university and the Fashion Arts Academy, he turned his creative thought to personal investment strategies. After earning his credentials, his career as Professor of Finance and Marketing for 25 years culminated in the revolutionary book, <u>The Profit-Taker Breakthrough: the Proven Rapid Money-Maker in Good & Bad Markets</u>. Don has conducted Profit-Taker Seminars in the United States and Canada at leading universities and colleges. The seminars are repeatedly sold out. He has been interviewed on over 100 television and radio programs and a television series based on his investment philosophy attracted large audiences.

For further information concerning Profit-Taker Seminars in your area please contact Hedge Publishers. (front page).